C000231466

BISON
BOOKS

Speaking of Indians

BY

ELLA DELORIA

Introduction to the Bison Books Edition
by Vine Deloria Jr.

UNIVERSITY OF NEBRASKA PRESS
LINCOLN AND LONDON

Introduction © 1998 by the University of Nebraska Press
Manufactured in the United States of America

⊛ The paper in this book meets the minimum requirements
of American National Standard for Information Sciences—
Permanence of Paper for Printed Library Materials,
ANSI Z39.48-1984.

First Bison Books printing: 1998
Most recent printing indicated by the last digit below:
10   9   8   7   6   5   4   3   2   1

Library of Congress Cataloging-in-Publication Data
Deloria, Ella Cara.
Speaking of Indians / by Ella Deloria; introduction to the
Bison Books edition by Vine Deloria Jr.
p. cm.
Originally published: New York: Friendship Press, 1944.
ISBN 0-8032-6614-6 (pbk.: alk. paper)
1. Teton Indians.   2. Dakota Indians.   I. Deloria, Vine.
II. Title.
E99.T34D45   1998
970′.004′97—dc21
98-19607   CIP

Reprinted from the original 1944 edition by Friendship
Press, New York.

ACKNOWLEDGMENT

My thanks are due to all who have read my manuscript and offered constructive suggestions. Especially would I thank Miss Edith M. Dabb, former missionary teacher and for many years Y. W. C. A. secretary for Indian work, whose criticisms out of a breadth of knowledge and a wealth of experience were most helpful to me.

I am profoundly grateful to the Missionary Education Movement for giving me this chance to speak out freely from the Indian's point of view. The widest latitude was allowed me, with the apparent confidence that I would be able to set forth some problems, not always plain to outsiders, which beset the Indian people in their efforts to progress. If I have justified that confidence in some measure, I am glad.

ELLA DELORIA

New York City
May, 1944

INTRODUCTION

Vine Deloria Jr.

This book was written during World War II as one of several books by or about American Indians and published by the Friendship Press in New York, then affiliated with the National Council of Churches. In many ways it is a popularization of much more complex ideas with which Ella Deloria was working in her more scholarly activities. The many white Americans who had an interest in Indians held determined stereotypes about Indian life, and the image of the savage still held sway with many of them. Added to that burden was the rigid idea that Indians needed Christianity in order to achieve anything in American society. G. E. E. Lindquist, zealously committed to showing that the "Jesus Road" was the only value possessed by Indians, had dominated the church publication field with his works for several decades. It is a tribute to the people of Friendship Press that they took this step forward in allowing Ella, Ruth Muskrat Bronson, and others to write favorable books about Indians.

Ella's path to authoring this book took many strange twists and turns. Her father, my grandfather, was the son of a very powerful medicine man—Saswe. His grandfather in turn was a French trapper who had married into a band of Yanktonais in the 1780s. So there was some mixture of European blood in the family. Saswe had a powerful vision that determined the course of our family for the next four generations. Philip, Ella's father, accompanied his father when he went to heal people and so was saturated with the experience of otherworldly things from an early age. When still a teenager Philip determined to convert to Christianity. His father had foreseen the permanent occupation of Sioux lands by the invading whites and had counseled Philip that the people had to make an accommodation to the new ways or perish. Saswe even resigned from his position as chief of band Eight of the Yankton tribe and took up farming and cutting and selling wood to the steamboats traveling up the Missouri.

Philip and two other young Sioux, Baptiste Lambert and David Tatiyopa, organized a "Planting Society" to encourage the Yanktons to accommodate themselves to the new way of life. Philip was then chosen to replace his father as chief of the band, a position he held until well into this century. But Philip realized that without some education in the white man's ways, he could not be effective in adjusting to the new ways himself. So he converted to Christianity and was sent to two boarding schools to be educated. Eventually, he returned to the Yankton Reservation as a church worker at Choteau Creek. He married quite young and was blessed with a son, but his happiness did not last long. His wife died of influenza, and his son was stricken with tuberculosis at the age of six and perished.

Philip married again and this time was blessed with a boy and two girls, but tragedy struck again. His wife died, and the boy soon followed her, leaving him with two young girls. He was almost beyond help from grief and perhaps had severe misgivings about his commitment to the white man's way but continued to work as a missionary. Philip then married my grandmother, Mary, herself a widow with two young daughters. Ella was the first child of this union. Philip, looking around at the five girls he now had as a family, despaired of fulfilling Saswe's vision of four generations of sons to work out the family responsibility of the vision. So

Ella, during her formative years, became the inheritor of the traditions of the family and was treated as if she were the son to whom Philip could pass down the stories.

Philip and Mary had then a boy, Philip Uyllesses; another girl, Susan; and finally my father, Vine, who was something of an afterthought apparently, since there were twelve years between him and Ella. In many ways, Ella was a mother rather than a sister to my father. More important, during her very young years she was acquainted with many of the elders at Standing Rock and Yankton Reservations and learned firsthand from them the old Sioux ways. Many of these people had passed on by the time my father and Susan were old enough to listen to the stories of elders visiting in their home.

A testimony to Ella's traditional upbringing is the fact that when she died she had all her teeth, not a cavity among them, and could still open a pop bottle with her jaws and teeth—a trick she only occasionally performed. The foods of her childhood gave her an incredibly healthy body from the very beginning. At the age of twelve Ella was driving a team of horses for her father and something spooked them, causing the team to bolt and run away. The wagon tipped, and Ella was injured. She lost her right thumb in the accident, a misfortune that plagued her the rest of her life and hampered her typing skills considerably.

But no other misfortunes befell her, and Philip relied on her to take care of the younger children and serve as surrogate son. Many of the stories that my father and my aunt Susie knew about the old days were given to them by Ella, not by their father. When Philip Uyllesses died suddenly at the age of 10, Philip went into a deep despair over the possibility of the vision ever being realized, and Ella, barely twelve, had to rally her father from his depression.

Strangely, Philip's mother and several older family relatives lived to be quite old, so Ella knew many things from the very olden times. I tried one time to get her to talk about these things, but she got very angry and told me that these things were so precious to the old people that my generation would not appreciate them and should not know them. They should not be talked about by people who cannot understand, she argued, and so when she died an immense body of knowledge went with her.

Like many other missionary daughters, Ella became a student at Bishop Hare's All Saints School in Sioux Falls, South Dakota. Bishop Hare had made great inroads in converting members of the Sioux tribe. He had more than twenty Sioux priests—people who had converted to Christianity early in their lives, served countless years as deacons, and were finally made priests in their later years. The pay for Indian priests was miniscule—since they were not seminary-trained—and educating their children was one way the church could compensate for the low salaries. Ella spent four years at All Saints and showed such an aptitude for absorbing the white man's knowledge that she received church support to attend the University of Chicago and later Oberlin College in Ohio. Oberlin must have made quite an impression on Ella, since I remember she always felt warmly toward it although she spent but a short time there. She then attended Columbia University in New York City, where she received a Bachelor of Science degree in June 1915. At Columbia she met Franz Boas, the prominent anthropologist and linguist with whom she was destined to work sporadically until his death in 1942.

Ella's mother died in the late summer of 1916, causing quite a disruption of the family. My father was quickly sent to the Kearney Military School in Nebraska, an early

Episcopal Church effort to provide a better education for its members in the Great Plains. Susan was having severe health problems, which were diagnosed later as small benign brain tumors that eventually had to be removed surgically. My grandfather began to decline in health also. Losing his third wife shook his faith in the religion he had so energetically tried to follow, and he began to turn more and more to the old ways. Ella had to pick up the burden of family leadership and, without causing any hard feelings, try to keep everyone functioning well.

Had Philip been able to function as he once had, there is no question that he would have found church funds to see that Ella was able to do graduate work. But his concern now was with my father and with his grandchildren, whom he wanted near him. Susan went to Chicago to study art, but her illness frequently caused her to miss classes and fail to remember her assignments. It started to become clear that someone would have to provide for her most of her adult life. She became increasingly self-conscious and hesitant to appear in public, eventually with anyone except old and close friends. So Ella was trapped with family responsibilities at the very time she should have been embarking on a professional life.

Ella had several short-term projects with the YWCA and received an appointment to initiate a special program in physical education at Haskell Indian School, where she spent three years. In 1927 she produced a pageant, "Indian Progress: Commemorating a Half Century of Endeavor among the Indians of North America," which was performed by students at the homecoming celebration that year. It was very mild by today's standards and simply demonstrated that Indians could adapt to the most rigorous (and nonsensical) requirements of white society. The following year she began work with Franz Boas, checking the accuracy and translations of the George Bushotter materials and Stephen Riggs's Dakota dictionary. Contrary to the contentions of some modern scholars, Ella spoke all three dialects of the Sioux language, although she was most familiar with the "d" dialect. She had picked up great fluency in the "l" dialect from her late childhood years at Wakpala among the Hunkpapas and Blackfeet Sioux. A year later she published a paper on the "Sun Dance of the Oglala Sioux," in the *Journal of American Folklore*. It was her first real venture into scholarly writing, and she identified several more ceremonies among the Tetons than the traditional seven identified by white scholars. She was very hesitant about getting into the religious field because Philip was suffering a series of strokes and becoming regretful of the passing of the old days, and she did not want to increase his emotional burden.

Her work with Boas continued but hardly offered a steady salary with any sense of security. Boas apparently raised funds to support Ella's work on an ad-hoc basis, and she was always short of funds to support herself and Susan. In fact the two of them were reduced to selling their trust land along the way to gain some kind of income when times were sparse. Nevertheless, her work with Boas finally bore fruit. In 1932 *Dakota Texts*, which included stories of the old days and line-by-line translations, was published. Ella did not like this kind of translation, which suggested that words and ideas could be easily matched across complex linguistic traditions. She felt a better rendering of the nuances of the Sioux language could be achieved by translating whole phrases and speeches in a free form. Sometimes when she and Susan would visit us she would get to talking about how certain things that had been translated word for word missed the point altogether.

Ella and Boas coauthored an article on Sioux linguistics, "Notes on Dakota Teton Dialect," which was published in the *International Journal of American Linguistics* in 1933. It appeared that her scholarly work would now enter a new phase where she could get some national recognition and perhaps some financial support to continue her study of the Sioux dialects. But her family had fallen apart. The death of her half sister Lima brought the need to care for four children left motherless, and Philip died in 1931. My father, a young priest just entering the Episcopal ministry, was fighting with the Episcopal bishop, who wanted to pay him half the salary a priest made because he was an Indian. So he could do little to solve the family financial difficulties. Ella and Susan visited our home several times during the mid-1930s, staying until Boas could send some money or Ella could get paying speaking assignments.

In 1938–39 Ella was one of four people asked to conduct a study of the Navajos sponsored by the Phelps-Stokes Fund and the Bureau of Indian Affairs. This project, eventually published as a report entitled *The Navajo Indian Problem*, opened the door for more speaking activities for her, and Boas was able to find additional funds to help her continue her language work. I spent a couple of weeks with Ella and Susan at Fort Lee, New Jersey, in 1939 just after the Navajo project was concluded. They took me to the 1939 World's Fair in New York City and nearly walked me to death trying to show me the exhibits. At that time Ella was still hoping to devote her energies to the Sioux language projects, and I had to sit quietly on the doorstep of their apartment in the afternoons while she worked in the other room.

In 1940 Ella was asked by the Bureau of Indian Affairs to go to Pembroke, North Carolina, to conduct studies of the Lumbee Indians. The bureau had started to recognize this community as Indians who should be under federal supervision, but their history had become entangled with a variety of myths that made recognition very difficult. Rumor since then has it that bureau anthropologists measured the heads of individuals, and those whose cranial dimensions corresponded with the measurements done earlier on Blackfeet Indians of Montana were recognized as being Tuscaroras. A community was started for them under the resettlement program, and I understand that some of these people still live on the lands purchased for them.

Ella and Susan produced two pageants for the Lumbees in 1940 and 1941. The productions were very successful, and older Lumbees today still remember them. The storylines followed then-popular wisdom of Lumbee origins and suggested that they had within their community remnants of Sir Walter Raleigh's "Lost Colony." About ten years ago I went to Pembroke and discovered that an old Lumbee couple had the original copy of one of the pageants. Through intermediaries, I asked if I could have it so copies could be made and the original could be kept at Pembroke State University for the Lumbee people. They had been Ella and Susan's landlords during the times they spent in North Carolina and showed me the little house my aunts had rented. As to the copy of the pageant, however, I was stymied. "Miss Ella said to keep this safe until she returned," I was told in no uncertain terms, and they refused to show it to me. I tried to explain that "Miss Ella" had died in 1971 and was not going to return, and that as her nephew I was in charge of her literary estate. But Ella had put the fear of God into them, and they truly believed that big New York producers would try and get the manuscript away and produce it up north. So as far as I know it still resides in some mysterious location in a Pembroke attic.

Ella was fascinated with the Lumbees, and I believe if she had lived to give testimony on their behalf when they were seeking federal recognition she would have been a powerful witness. When I was in the Marines at Quantico, Virginia, I happened to talk to Ella about the Lumbee research when she visited me on her way back north from Pembroke. Ella deeply believed that she could have reconstructed the original Indian language spoken by these people. She said that she spent as much time as possible with the Lumbee women and quizzed them about the names of plants, the kinds of food they cooked, the names used for the different animals, and the folk medicines they used. Tracing back from the colloquial expressions of these women and then comparing their slang words with words in other Indian tongues, she was preparing a sophisticated dictionary that she believed was very close to their original language before English words and phrases were added. She had over three hundred words identified on little index cards and was thinking of revisiting Pembroke before more elders passed away. These cards, as well as copious notes on the Sioux language, were stored in two steamer trunks in Fort Lee when Ella and Susan went west in 1944. Unfortunately, she never had enough money to pay the storage bill, and the space she had was closed and her things sold—probably for the value of the steamer trunks. Much of her scholarly production was lost.

In 1943 Ella received the Indian Achievement Award from the Indian Council Fire in Chicago. At the time this was the most prestigious award an Indian could receive, but it did not translate into career advancement. Boas had died the previous year and her only continuing source of support had vanished with him. During the late 1940s and early 1950s Ella and Susan lived pretty much hand to mouth, with Ella taking many short-term teaching and

workshop jobs to eke out a living. Some funds were forthcoming from the American Philosophical Society and the
Viking Fund, allowing Ella to devote some time and en-
ergy to working on a new manuscript, *Dakota Family Life:
Social Patterns and Education,* which is actually a greatly
expanded and secular version of the discussion of kin and
family presented in this book.

In 1955 Ella and Susan were hired by the Episcopal
Church to operate the St. Elizabeth's Mission Home at
Wakpala, South Dakota, where Philip had been priest for
nearly forty years. It was a bittersweet reunion with friends
of their childhood. Conditions were now greatly changed.
Wakpala had diminished considerably; many people were
now dead, and even more had moved away. Although they
were at St. Elizabeth's for a little over three years, the experience seemed to change both of them radically. They began
to talk mostly about the old days and to spend more time
touring South Dakota visiting with relatives.

In 1961 Ella went to the University of South Dakota
and served as assistant director of the W. H. Over Mu-
seum, doing work on the Sioux dialects. The University
received a grant in 1962 for Ella to work on a Santee
Sioux dictionary. In 1963 Susan died, and Ella was finally freed of her family obligations, although at an age
when she could do little. She served on various national
committees and organizations and was particularly active in work at St. Mary's School for Indian Girls, the last
operating church mission school of the Episcopal Church.
During these final years, Ella continued to make trips to
the isolated settlements on the different reservations to
contact elders who could remember the old words and
phrases. I talked to her after one exhausting trip to Red
Shirt Table on the Pine Ridge Reservation, and she said,
"Research is getting so hard to do—there are hardly any

elders around nowadays." I pointed out that she was now one of the surviving elders and the chances of discovering a crowd of ninety-year-olds were steadily declining. She just gave me a disgusted look, as she refused to consider herself an elder.

After experiencing a series of strokes and related ailments, Ella died on February 12, 1971, at Wagner, South Dakota, not far from where she had been born. As might have been expected, she left a few trunks and boxes stored in different locations, and although my father did his best to collect them, we were never certain that there were not treasures of manuscripts somewhere. Ella was buried at St. Philip's Church near Lake Andes along with Susan; her mother, Mary; her grandmother; and an assortment of sisters and aunts. In death as in life Ella was surrounded by family.

Speaking of Indians is written in a style compatible with the expectations of the church audiences for which the book was intended. So it does have very optimistic statements about Christianity and the need for it among the Sioux. Hidden within the propaganda, however, is Ella's effort to describe the positive aspects of the old Sioux culture and kinship. Many examples used in this book can be easily identified since they are taken from Ella's circles of friends and relatives. I like best the reference to Indians watching the Flyer train speeding across the country. In her belongings I found a picture of the people at Wakpala sitting on the hillside watching a fast train speed through the reservation. It is dated 1903, when Ella was just reaching adolescence, and I suspect she was the photographer, recording behavior even at that early age.

CONTENTS

Part I

THIS MAN CALLED INDIAN

Part II

"A SCHEME OF LIFE THAT WORKED"

Part III

THE RESERVATION PICTURE

Part IV

THE PRESENT CRISIS

SPEAKING OF INDIANS

They were neither yelling demon nor Noble Savage.
They were a people.
                              A people not yet fused,
Made one into a whole nation, but beginning
As the Gauls began, or the Britons that Caesar found.
As the Greeks began, in their time.
          .   .   .   .

They were a people, beginning—
                              With beliefs,
Ornaments, language, fables, love of children
(You will find that spoken of in all the books.)
And a scheme of life that worked.

                              —Stephen Vincent Benét [1]

[1] From *Western Star,* copyright 1943 by Farrar & Rinehart, Inc. Used by permission.

Part I

This Man Called Indian

1: THE INDIAN ENTERS AMERICA

SCIENCE TELLS US THAT THE NATIVE AMERICANS came from northern Asia and that they may have arrived here from ten to twelve thousand years ago. But they were not the first inhabitants of this continent. From archeological evidences we know that man-made implements of stone were left beside ancient campfires fifteen to eighteen thousand years ago, some even say twenty thousand. Man-made projectiles, too, have been found deep in the earth, together with the skeletons of a prehistoric species of bison. It is known from such remains that these earlier peoples lived by both hunting and seed-gathering. We cannot know what became of them—whether they had all vanished before the ancestors of the modern Indians arrived, or whether some were still wandering about and were absorbed by the newcomers. Of course, every bit of this is speculative; one guess is nearly as good as another, for we can never be sure of what actually took place.

And it doesn't really matter, does it? All that which lies hidden in the remote past is interesting, to be sure, but not so important as the present and the future. The vital concern is not where a people came from, physically, but where they are going, spiritually. Even so, it does help to look briefly at these theories of origins.

We all know that the natives of America are not really Indians, that that name was mistakenly applied to them by Columbus when he reached these shores and supposed he had found India by sailing west. Then who are they? Scientists generally give as the best answer possible with the evidence now in hand that the ancestry of the Indians is Mongoloid. This does not mean that the Indians are Chinese nor that they came from China—for the excellent reason that at the assumed period of their arrival in America China and the Chinese were not yet in existence. Old as they are, the Chinese, by comparison, are recent. It is more nearly true to say that the Indians probably have a remote ancestry in common with other Asiatic peoples of today. But it was all so very long ago and the various races of mankind—which presumably had a common biological origin—have become so differentiated that no one knows what racial intermixtures may have occurred during the long ages.

It is supposed that the migrations from Asia that began ten to twelve thousand years ago took place in waves with varying intervals between. When they ended no one knows, or what finally put a stop to them. Perhaps it was some drastic change of climate or topography. Look on a map at the vast expanse of northern Asia stretching eastward all the way from old Russia and northeastward from the China of today to the point where it almost meets America, with only the narrow straits to hold the old and new worlds apart. It is not hard to imagine that small bands of hunters broke away occasionally from the tribes that roamed there and gradually found their way into the new world, either by boat or perhaps by a land bridge that later disappeared.

The newcomers brought with them the knowledge and progress of their people back home in what we now call Siberia. It was not much, in that remote age—the early New Stone Age, sometimes called the Neolithic Age. They brought along the throwing stick; stone implements and tools, better made than those of the first Stone Age, but very simple still; a knowledge of basket-making; probably with the first migration, the bow and arrow; and only one domestic animal, the dog.

I can picture that dog, pulling a small travois on which are piled his master's few belongings. I can picture a line of early men, women, and children, struggling along on foot, and, among them, these burdened dogs. Snow and winds harshly whip across their primitive faces. All are heading for America, to become unwittingly the First Americans. If one stops to muse on them coming thus, one must feel a little sorry for them, for they were walking deliberately into a trap. With each step they were cutting themselves off for thousands of years from the rest of mankind.

Until they left home, no doubt their chances of progress were about even with those of other peoples. All human progress was slow at the beginning, but at least it was cumulative as long as peoples could occasionally get in touch with each other. But now, upon reaching the New World, the Indians began to lag behind, although it must be said to their credit that they never stood still. But why did they have to lag at all? The answer is easy, and happily it casts no reflection on their potentialities. They lagged because they were isolated. All progress depends on contacts and the resulting exchange of new ideas. Dr. Franz Boas has said:

We must bear in mind that none of these [ancient civilizations] was the product of the genius of a single people. Ideas and inventions were carried from one to the other; and so, although intercommunication was slow, each people which participated in that ancient development contributed its share to the general progress. Proofs without number are forthcoming to show that ideas have been disseminated for as long as people have come in contact with one another, and that neither race nor language nor distance limits their diffusion. As all races have worked together in the development of civilization, we must bow to the genius of all, whatever group of mankind they may represent.[1]

[1] *The Mind of Primitive Man,* by Franz Boas, pp. 6-7. New York, The Macmillan Co., 1922. Used by permission.

How true! But, alas, for thousands of years it was the destiny of the Indian to be deprived of a share in that exchange which flourished elsewhere in the world. What, then, could his progress be but slow? He had no neighboring peoples to stimulate him to make endeavors matching theirs. When we realize that, it is remarkable that all by himself and through his own genius he managed to achieve anything to add to the world's knowledge. And that suggests once more what we know already—that imagination and inventiveness are common human potentialities. All people invent.

This matter of independent development here in the Western world raises a logical question: Why the seeming disparity among the Indian peoples themselves? For it is true that some groups attained to high civilizations in what is now Mexico, Central America, and Peru, while others lived a barbaric existence, all simultaneously. According to the best scientific opinion, all the native Americans are one race. Even so, within any given race, progress is never uniform for all the people, because circumstances and life situations are never uniform. In the case of the prehistoric Indians, those tribes that lived entirely mobile lives in order to hunt and gather berries and seeds could never stay put long enough to start building together anything solid and lasting. Their culture necessarily remained static— and admirably suited to their simple needs.

And then there were other tribes that eventually worked their way to regions where the opportunities for obtaining food direct from nature were soon ex-

hausted, making a more settled and systematic agricu-
tural life an economic necessity. Such peoples were
obliged to stay close together and to work out a new
way of life. After a while they were building cities,
accumulating wealth, and discovering and inventing
things to better their material existence.

The civilizations of the Incas, Aztecs, Toltecs, and
Mayas were really quite wonderful. We should all
know more about them, if for no other reason than that
they were so purely American in origin. A good account of them reads like a fairy tale. It sounds incredible that some of the same primitive peoples who had
stumbled accidentally onto this continent only a few
thousand years earlier should have wrought such civilizations—comparable to those of the ancient world, and
all without foreign help. Yet that is what they did.

I cannot resist giving a few of the achievements and
the inventions and discoveries independently made
here. Weaving, pottery, metalwork and other art;
architectural and engineering works, such as roads,
mounds, and pyramids, capped by temples to the gods;
cities with streets and street lights; waterworks and
spouting fountains in the gardens of the rich; complicated religious and judicial systems and codified
laws; schools for boys and girls; a knowledge of mathe-
matics and of astronomy, about like that known in the
Old World, before Copernicus; and, perhaps most important of all, a system of writing. Thanks to that,
records were kept regularly; and if we had them all
today, we might know even more about that indigenous

culture so vital and fresh. But, unfortunately, the Spaniards destroyed most of them, as works of Satan.

But now, while remembering those great civilizations to the south and being properly impressed by them, we need to keep in mind the wild tribes of the same race that through the centuries were still roaming about up north, hunting, gathering the fruits of the earth, and fishing—all in the same old way. Those tribes were made up of vastly different men—men whose outlook and habits of life were a far cry from the more advanced peoples farther south. Do you recall the story of the Roman orator who cautioned his friend, "Do not obtain your slaves from Britain, because they are so stupid and so utterly incapable of being taught that they are not fit to form part of the household of Athens"?

We smile at that, remembering Britain today. Well, there might easily have been a comparable case, wherein some Aztec gentleman warned his friend, "Do not obtain your help from those awful, wild tribes in the far north [the Dakotas, for example!], because they are so stupid and so utterly incapable of being taught that they are not fit to form part of the household of Tenochtitlan."

Even if there was a time when Britain was trailing so far behind the civilized world that Roman and Greek nobles could with impunity talk slightingly of her people, she did not stay there. Is it not thinkable that those wild Indian tribes of the north could likewise have caught up, if only they had had another long period of normal growth in which to emerge from a hunting to a settled, farming economy, and then to build a material civilization like that of the Aztecs and the rest?

Why not? Scientists say that the native Americans differ in no essential particular from the rest of mankind. And it is now well established that all human beings in the world are biologically one family.

"This means, in concrete terms, that however different the customs of the people you may come in contact with, they could have been very much like yourself in habits and outlook, except for the accident of location and upbringing." So writes Dr. Gene Weltfish, Columbia University anthropologist, in an article preparing our soldiers to meet new peoples the world over with intelligence and understanding.

According to that, the Indian had it in him to progress in his own way quite as much as the Briton in his. And I believe he could have done so if his normal life had not been suddenly disrupted, and if he had not been forced to make so drastic a change in his methods and his direction.

At a leisurely pace, the Indians would have gone on learning from one another. Discoveries and inventions at the centers of progress would have worked outward until they had reached every tribe. Students of Indian history have established that, by the fifteenth century of our era, certain cultural elements had already been spreading. The most obvious were those related to agriculture. Knowledge of the cultivation of corn, beans, squashes, and other crops had reached most of the tribes. Even the most mobile of them had learned to grow corn.

Do we realize that these agricultural products were developed by the Indians? From a wild plant with a tiny ear came maize; from a species of the wild cucumber vine came squashes and pumpkins, and so on. These were all indigenous plants, for we are told that no seed was carried here from Asia.

Within that same era ideas and arts were also passing from tribe to tribe—a knowledge of building, for example, apparent today in the ruins left behind by the prehistoric cliff builders, as well as various forms of art expression. All human beings learn from each other, we have been saying. The Indians, belonging to the great human family, have the same innate powers, inborn intelligence, and potentialities as the rest of mankind. They have imagination and inventiveness. They can copy what they see and adapt it to their own special needs. These are all common human traits. The Indians in the long centuries through which they spread out over two continents were only running true to their nature. They had their own aims and their own methods for achieving them; and those aims and methods were the direct outgrowth of their peculiar situation and life circumstances. They differed in their habits and outlook simply because they were not exposed to the influences of outside cultures.

Otherwise, they were just some more of earth's peoples climbing.

2: TRIBAL LANGUAGES AND CULTURE AREAS

WITH THE COMING OF THE WHITE MAN, THE IN-dian's existence became suddenly known to the rest of the world, and his situation and life circumstances came under close observation. In this chapter we shall look at two important aspects of his life that have been widely studied: his language or, more accurately, his languages; and his material culture.

From such evidences as are available scientists have been able to conjecture, with what they regard as reasonable accuracy, much as to the Indian's prehistoric life in its prehistoric setting. These are complex and involved matters, too much so for a detailed examination of them in this brief introduction to Indian life. But, if we can fix in mind a few points that are basic for a working knowledge, the rest can wait.

Let's consider language. In the first place, don't you think it rather amazing that so few people, relatively, should have developed so many different languages in the New World? Where did they all come from, these only real American languages? Well, we can offer a reasonable answer to that one.

Briefly, this is what must have happened. Each migrating group of those first peoples came speaking whatever language was spoken back home in Siberia, of course. Very probably they soon separated into small

groups, the better to find their food. As the years and
the centuries passed they lost track of one another forever; but they were all still using a common tongue.

As each division of any one large original group met
new experiences, however, and had new ideas to express, new words were coined and new forms and speech
devices introduced. Perhaps, too, they occasionally met
up with another people stemming from another migration and of course using an entirely different language; and they borrowed a word from them now and
then. By some such means, each of the original tongues
underwent constant modification in two ways: it
changed from its original character, and it also
changed from all its sister divisions. Originally, that is,
for each large migration group the language was one;
but in time, after dividing and subdividing and changing in as many directions as there were divisions and
subdivisions of that original group, it became many
languages. At first they were only as different as dialects are; but, after thousands of years, they became
mutually unintelligible. Thus the later peoples, which
had become large tribes meantime, felt no kinship with
one another because they could not understand one another's speech. It was not strange then that such tribes,
though linguistically related, came to regard one another as enemies, and often carried on at least sporadic
warfare. Remember, I am not saying categorically that
this is what happened. But something like it surely did.

Here are a few facts that may be remembered easily.
Linguistic scholars have been able to identify over one

hundred and fifty distinct languages spoken north of
Mexico. They have examined these languages critically
and noted that certain ones resemble each other fundamentally in their possession of definite common traits.
They have therefore grouped the languages into families, or language stocks, according to these traits, and
have given them family names for convenience in dis-
cussing and studying them. The names are more or
less arbitrary. They are *not* the names of those mother
tongues of ten thousand and more years ago, because
nobody knows what they were. Here are some of the
language stocks that include many of the languages
of North America whose names are quite familiar:
Siouan, Iroquoian, Algonquian, Athapascan, Musk-
hogean, Uto-Aztecan, and—that is enough, for now.
The numbers within each stock vary. The Siouan family, for instance, has around twenty languages whose
names, at least, are on record. Nobody knows how
many more have passed unrecognized from the scene
with the peoples that spoke them. The Zuñi language,
on the other hand, is unique in that it bears no relationship to any other language.

Now a word about language "scatter." In the central United States there are a dozen or more tribes
speaking languages found to be cognates, from which
it is inferred reasonably that once they must have been
one people. But they did not know this; and often
fought one another in the past. These languages are all
Siouan. But that is not all. Down in the Gulf states
two more Siouan languages were found, the Biloxi and

the Ofo, though they are now practically extinct. And
then, on the Atlantic coast, there were still other cognates. Those Eastern Siouan tongues were once alive
and active, used by thirty-six or more dialect groups,
principally over the Carolinas and dipping into Virginia, before and during early Colonial times. Inci-
dentally, all those Eastern Siouan-speaking peoples
have vanished, except for a very small remnant of
Catawbas in South Carolina. Thus we can see that,
whatever the "Siouan" mother tongue may have been,
her children certainly got around. Similar wide scat-
ters of other families have been charted.

We have tried to see the American languages in
their larger aspects; now let's look at them in more
detail. One mark of the human family, which sets them
forever apart from other animals, is their ability to
communicate their thoughts through the medium of
speech. Some languages are regarded as highly developed, others as limited and poor. Before Indian languages were critically studied the general opinion was
that they were hopelessly inadequate and could express
only the simplest wants. Actually, however, the type
of language used by at least some of the tribes assures
them a decent rung on the intellectual ladder.

What are they like? Well, the ones I know are rich
and full of vitality, picturesque, laconic, and capable
of subtle shades of meaning. It was a white man's joke,
now worn rather thin, that all an Indian could do to
express himself was to grunt. "Ugh!" was supposed to
be his whole vocabulary. But the opposite is true.

14   SPEAKING OF INDIANS

There is, to begin with, that sizable Dakota dictionary compiled by Stephen Riggs over sixty years ago in the Santee-Dakota dialect, and also the English-Dakota dictionary, a later work, by John P. Williamson. Since then other missionaries have also made more or less extensive vocabularies for their own use from the dialects of particular groups. I am told of one such list that now contains twenty-five thousand words. In my own investigations I have amassed so many words in the four Dakota dialects—Yankton, Santee, Teton, and Assiniboin—that I despair of ever classifying them and making them available for the use of students in linguistics.

Those who really know and speak Indian languages can tell you that they are quite adequate and elastic enough to meet not only ordinary needs but also extraordinary ones as they appear. Each language, moreover, has its own complicated but perfectly rational grammatical structure governed by specific rules. Dr. Edward Kennard, anthropologist in the Indian Service and specialist in languages, calls it a "naïve assumption" that primitive languages lack words for new ideas, and he observes that European languages lacked technical terms until the need for them arose.[2]

I have one pretty fine illustration of the point. A young Dakota woman, who for only a short time in her

[2] See "The Use of Native Languages and Cultures in Indian Education," by Edward A. Kennard, in *The Changing Indian,* edited by Oliver LaFarge, pp. 113-114. Norman, University of Oklahoma Press, 1942.

childhood had attended one of the mission schools, was called on to interpret for a sick friend.

"Tell Mrs. Lamont to relax, Emma," the physician said to her. The young woman frowned, groping for a way to convey that request, for there is no specific word that exactly expresses "relax." But almost immediately she came up with a word, and it was admirably right.

"*T'a-t'a-ic'i-ya!*" she told the sick woman. It analyzes thus: *t'a* means to be dead; doubled *t'a-t'a* means to be continuously dead, dead-in-process like an old melon or potato, or flabbily dead like a withered member; *ic'i-* is the reflexive; *ya* means to cause. What she really said was, "Cause-yourself-to-be-paralyzed." I needn't add that the sick woman relaxed instantly.

That was quick thinking and resourcefulness. Yet it was not a unique thing she did. That sort of word-making is quite possible in Dakota; and it comes natural to users of languages having that capacity. Of course, not every speaker does it with equal felicity, because it depends also on imagination—a variable power in any race. Only the keen, clever minds can consistently do it with the best effect. A magnetic Dakota orator is one who, possessed of the other necessary qualities, has in addition unusual skill in this respect. But sometimes even the most prosaic come out with words that surprise and delight you by their aptness.

Our other subject in this chapter I said was to be material culture. In studying that side of Indian life, scholars find it convenient to make a geographical classification and to group together the tribes belonging to each "culture area," irrespective of language differences.[3] Here I shall not need to repeat the detailed descriptions of these areas as given by students of anthropology, but simply list some random ideas and phrases that are familiar to many of us in our American history and folklore:

1. *Southeastern.* Dugout canoes—stockaded villages—a real caste system—best defined political organization—the Pocahontas and John Smith idyll.

2. *Eastern Woodlands.* Iroquois League—the long house—ceremonial masks carved from the living tree—Hiawatha—Handsome Lake's Code—the Peace Tree.

3. *Plains.* The good old buffalo—the sun dance—expert horsemanship—intertribal warfare for glory and sport—the tipi—the Sioux war bonnet of eagle feathers—fringed buckskin garments.

4. *Plateau.* Weakest area for social organization—a medley of culture traits spilling over into it from surrounding areas having better defined cultures.

5. *Southwestern.* Ancient pueblo life—Navajo shepherds—rugs and turquoise jewelry—the snake dance—"sings" for healing—sand painting—precise rituals.

6. *California.* Best in basketry technique—rabbitskin robes—seed-gathering for subsistence—acorns the staple food.

[3] See "Cultural Backgrounds," by Erna Gunther, Chapter II of *The Indian in American Life,* by G. E. E. Lindquist and collaborators. New York, Friendship Press, 1944.

7. *North Pacific Coast.* The totem pole—the "potlatch"—salmon fishing—social prestige dependent on wealth.

Some such scheme is a help in keeping clear in one's mind a comprehensive view of the entire Indian scene in North America and in gaining a fairly definite idea of the several types of culture.

But we have to be careful not to assume that even within those areas the same features prevail uniformly. Far from it! How could they, since each area contains several distinct tribes speaking diverse languages, thinking different thoughts, and having preferences for particular modes of life? We need to keep in mind, too, that the lines of demarcation are never clean cut. Imagine a patchwork quilt in which the scraps of cloth are, unfortunately, not of fast color. After one wash there would be a blurring out of tones, a blending of each two neighboring colors along the seams. That's about the way culture areas are. The world over, people borrow and adapt ideas when they have the chance. An illustration of this is the art of the Santee-Dakotas who occupy the eastern border of the Dakota domain. To the east of them were their Algonquian neighbors whose culture was Eastern Woodlands. Through their influence, Santee art is floral rather than geometric, like that of the rest of the Dakotas. In thought, too, and in ceremonies they resembled their Chippewa neighbors more than their fellow tribesmen to the west. Yet they are Dakotas; and Dakotas are classified as Plains in culture.

Even if a person knew nothing whatever about Indian languages and culture areas but what is contained in this chapter, I believe he would have a fair background against which to begin a study of Indians —but only to begin! For, of course, a glance at the legendary and conjectured past of a race and a light discussion of their vehicles of expression and their regionally varying forms of material culture do no more than open the door to an understanding of that race. There remains still in the life of every people something else, too significant to ignore.

3: SPIRITUAL CULTURE AREAS

WE MAY KNOW ABOUT A PEOPLE, BUT WE CANNOT truly know them until we can get within their minds, to some degree at least, and see life from their peculiar point of view. To do that we must learn what goes on in their "spiritual culture area." By that fancy phrase I simply mean what remains after the tangible and visible part is cleared away. I mean such ethical values and moral principles as a people discovers to live by and that make it a group distinct from its neighbors. I mean all those unseen elements that make up the mass sentiment, disposition, and character— elements that completely blend there, producing in an integrated pattern a powerful inner force that is in habitual operation, dictating behavior and controlling the thought of all who live within its sphere.

It is an elusive area, without any location that we can visit bodily. Like heaven, it is hard to define, delimit, and describe. And yet it is the "realest" part of a people, just as is the inner life of an individual. Somehow we have to get inside that area and explore with unprejudiced mind its workings, or we cannot understand the people who are the direct product of it.

We sometimes hear of the "fabric" of a culture as if it were woven of varicolored strands. If only it were! How easily we could pull out the red or the blue, and then examine one color after another. To me it is no simple woven fabric. It is not a fabric at all, really, but more like a marble cake. Dough in various colors— pink, green, brown—is mixed together and then baked. No matter where we lay our knife, we cut through every color, not once but many times. And that's the kind of thing I felt I had to talk about in this book. Since in every living culture all elements are interrelated, many aspects of life are bound to be mentioned repeatedly in these chapters, each time in reference to a varying set of factors.

It is relatively easy to understand all this interplay of cultural elements in a literate people, because they write about them and we can read. It is the unlettered peoples that present a problem, for they can only talk, and their words, howsoever lofty, are lost instantly. Language is indeed the gateway to their spiritual culture area, that "shrine of a people's soul." [4] To get

---

[4] I am indebted here to Dr. Edwin W. Smith for this phrase, which is the title of his valuable book on language.

at Indian thinking, then, requires effort in research and analysis; nevertheless, it is a saving in the end. And I believe it to be the first requisite for the work of our missionaries and our government.

What can I do, then, to help you understand the Indians? I could try to entertain you by skipping from tribe to tribe and giving you a surface picture of them all. I could give statistics and records and tell you about a "quaint custom," now and then, whenever I despair of holding your interest to the end. But I don't believe that is where my contribution lies. Instead of trying to cover the whole Indian scene, which many others can do ever so much better than I, I shall concentrate on the one people that I know intimately and whose language is also mine.

Parts II and III of this book will be on the Dakota people exclusively. In Part II we shall go back to a time prior to white settlement of the western plains, when native custom and thought were all there was, and we shall examine certain of the most significant elements in the old life. In Part III we shall come a bit nearer to the present and see what happened when a change was necessary: how the people made social, religious, educational, and economic adjustments to a new way when so much of the old had been irrevocably ended; and just what elements of the old are still persisting beyond their time.

And when we are through, your particular questions about Indians may still be unanswered. Out of this one situation there will not necessarily come the explanation of many problems deeply affecting other tribes. We in America must be realizing by now that too often all tribes, just because they are native Americans, are lumped together with blithe disregard of tribal differences. Do we lump together all Europeans just because they occupy the same continent? Don't we allow for the wide differences in the English, Russian, French, German temperaments? Right here in our own nation we recognize our regional differences. By what precedent, then, are all Indian tribes—speaking different languages and living different lives—expected to have the same ideas and problems? And to respond to exactly the same approach?

My people, the Dakotas, understood the meaning of self-sacrifice, perhaps because their legends taught them that the buffalo, on which their very life depended, gave itself voluntarily that they might live. A good ethnologist who has concentrated on another tribe, just as admirable as mine, tells me that they have no foundation for such an idea, either from their own past thought or in their mythology. Missionaries who would explain the Holy Eucharist in that particular tribe would, therefore, begin their task under the great handicap of having to introduce a completely foreign religious concept. Some tribes bow helpless before the Unseen, perhaps in pathetic fear and trembling; but at least they have a basis for Christian humility and reverence. But do you know that there is a tribe whose people have nothing of that—whose thought and mode of life on a stark desert shaped them in another way, so that to this day their priests go out arrogantly to meet their gods on an even footing with themselves? My tribe, as you will see, grasped—however crudely—the idea of self-immolation in prayer, even to scarifying themselves and suffering in other ways to show their earnest desires. There is another tribe that thinks that sort of thing is preposterous to the point of stupidity. According to one magazine writer, some of the members of this tribe laughed derisively when Hollywood, with characteristic nonchalance, tried to make Sioux of them by picturing them in such acts.

My tribe made almost a fetish of giving. When kindness was proffered by missionaries, they were sensitive to the spirit prompting it and knew how to respond. There is another tribe of entirely different tradition at this point. Among them anyone who offers something for nothing is a fool.

A few words on the background of the Dakotas are needed here. They are the second largest tribe and live principally in South Dakota. They divide naturally into three parts: those farthest east are the Santees; then come the Yanktons; and still farther west, beyond the Missouri, are the Tetons. They are all Dakotas, but they group on the basis of dialects. I am a Yankton and not a Teton; but, because my father was a missionary to them and I grew up among them, I am presenting a Teton picture primarily. The

Dakotas' contact with Christianity and civilization has been a westward-moving one, so that the Tetons were the last to be affected. Remember, please, that always there were more advanced Dakotas to the east of them.

Observe too, please, the historical perspective of the whole book.

In Part I, I have talked first about a shadowy and remote past in Asia, and then of the languages and material development of Indian peoples in North America down to the present.

In Part II, I touch only the Teton Dakotas as they lived before they were directly affected by white civilization. After the Dakotas obtained horses early in the eighteenth century the pace of tribal life quickened and radical changes resulted. I shall portray the lively culture existing at the height of the horse period, as I piece it together from stories handed down by word of mouth.

Part III starts roughly about 1890, when decisive events put an abrupt end to the old Teton life, making an adjustment to modern life not only wise but absolutely imperative. There was no other choice.

Part IV aims to concern itself once more with Indians in general—with all the tribes and their problems today, though an occasional illustration from the Dakotas is inevitable.

Part II

"A Scheme of Life That Worked"

4: KINSHIP'S RÔLE IN DAKOTA LIFE

ALL PEOPLES WHO LIVE COMMUNALLY MUST FIRST find some way to get along together harmoniously and with a measure of decency and order. This is a universal problem. Each people, even the most primitive, has solved it in its own way. And that way, by whatever rules and controls it is achieved, is, for any people, the scheme of life that works. The Dakota people of the past found a way: it was through kinship.

Kinship was the all-important matter. Its demands and dictates for all phases of social life were relentless and exact; but, on the other hand, its privileges and honorings and rewarding prestige were not only tolerable but downright pleasant and desirable for all who conformed. By kinship all Dakota people were held together in a great relationship that was theoretically all-inclusive and co-extensive with the Dakota domain.

Everyone who was born a Dakota belonged in it; nobody need be left outside. This meant that the Dakota camp-circles were no haphazard assemblages of heterogeneous individuals. Ideally, nobody living there was unattached. The most solitary member was sure to have at least one blood relative, no matter how distant, through whose marriage connections he was automatically the relative of a host of people. For, in Dakota society, everyone shared affinal relatives, that is, relatives-through-marriage, with his own relatives-through-blood.

Before going further, I can safely say that the ultimate aim of Dakota life, stripped of accessories, was quite simple: One must obey kinship rules; one must be a good relative. No Dakota who has participated in that life will dispute that. In the last analysis every other consideration was secondary—property, personal ambition, glory, good times, life itself. Without that aim and the constant struggle to attain it, the people would no longer be Dakotas in truth. They would no longer even be human. To be a good Dakota, then, was to be humanized, civilized. And to be civilized was to keep the rules imposed by kinship for achieving civility, good manners, and a sense of responsibility toward every individual dealt with. Thus only was it possible to live communally with success; that is to say, with a minimum of friction and a maximum of good will.

Let me try to explain the kinship system of the Dakotas as simply as I can, though it is complex at best. As a member of the tribe you have, of course, your

natural father and mother and siblings; that is, all
their other children, your brothers and sisters. So far
it is the same as in any other society. But now, in addition, there are any number of men and women whom
you also call father and mother, your secondary or
auxiliary parents. Those "fathers" are all the men
whom your own father calls brother or cousin. They
are not your uncles; only your mother's brothers and
cousins are your uncles. And those "mothers" are the
women whom your mother calls sister or cousin. They
are not your aunts; only your father's sisters and
cousins are your aunts.

Now you can see where you get so many other brothers and sisters besides your own, and where you get so
many cousins. These extended siblings and these cousins constitute your generation; you belong together.
Many of them live in your camp-circle, and many
others are sprinkled throughout the other Dakota
camp-circles moving over the land. Through them you
have actual and potential relatives practically everywhere you go.

You share affinal relatives, I said. This means that
when your blood relatives marry, all their new relatives
are yours, too; and, because your many secondary
fathers and mothers are of various ages—and some are
much older than your own parents—they may have
sons and daughters who are already married and parents themselves. Thus it happens that, through them,
you find yourself at birth with every kind of relative
a body could have: parents-in-law, sons and daughters,

nieces and nephews, and, in some cases, a grandchild or two—and of course, in that case, daughters-in-law and sons-in-law. All the spouses of all your siblings and cousins become your sisters- or brothers-in-law.

Because relationships through marriage extend practically ad infinitum, any strangers thrown together by circumstances are generally able to arrive at consistent terms for each other through some mutual relative, no matter how tortuous the path. It may sound artificial, and of course it was that, in the sense that it had to be devised. In the very remote situations, as between two persons who met only once or so in a lifetime, those terms were purely formal, but nonetheless essential, as we shall see.

Kinship ties being that important, blood connections were assiduously traced and remembered, no matter how far back, if only they could be definitely established. That was no easy feat either, since there were no records. However distant a relative might seem according to the white man's method of reckoning, he would be claimed by Dakotas.

Beyond all these relationships, which after all had a legitimate basis, there were still others that had to be established on a purely social basis. Ethnologists call this the social kinship system, as distinct from kinship based on blood and marriage. One's social kin then would be the same as one's friends, neighbors, and acquaintances in white society. Through this social kinship system even real outsiders became relatives.

My readers will be getting impatient just about here

and saying, "But why all this insistence on kinship and
kinship terms? Why all the artificial methods for
securing relatives? Why couldn't Dakotas simply be
friends, like other people?" So let's look at it from the
Dakota point of view.

All peoples have their own ways of showing courtesy.
The fundamental idea is the same: to be gracious and
kind and to show good will; to abide by the rules of
etiquette as practised by the majority, so as not to
appear boorish or queer. The idea is one; the methods
are many. Among the Dakotas it was rude to speak another's name boldly; one must employ the kinship term
instead. Not "Swift Cloud," but *"My uncle,* Swift
Cloud," or, where there was no danger of ambiguity,
simply "My uncle." Furthermore, it was improper to
plunge into conversation without first using the polite
term of kinship; only to animals might you speak so
rudely. Consequently, it was of the utmost importance
to know the right term for each person and not be
caught unaware. Naturally it followed that the right
terms of address were always the people's preoccupation.

This need of first establishing proper relationship
prevailed even when one came to pray. It gave a man
status with the Supernatural as well as with man. The
Dakota words "to address a relative" and "to pray"
are familiar everyday words. It was not until a few
years ago, when I was listing and defining verb-stems
for linguistic students at Columbia University, that
suddenly I realized that the two words are not really

two; they are one. *Wacekiya* means both acts. Nor is
that surprising, come to think of it, for a Dakota did
not like to deal with another person without first avow-
ing his own status, as a relative mindful of the duties
incumbent on him as such, while also reminding the
other of his. *Wacekiya* implies that in every meeting
of two minds the kinship approach is imperative; it is
the open-sesame to any sincere exchange of sentiment
between man and his neighbor or man and his God.
Once the channel is clear between the two, a reciprocal
trust and confidence are guaranteed. It is tantamount
to smoking the peace pipe; in fact, to smoke ceremonially is to *wacekiya*.

In other words, you simply did not dare have deal-
ings with strangers, because you could not be sure of
them. They might so easily turn out to be the incar-
nation of Iktomi, the legendary spirit of deceit, ready
to play a trick on you. Of relatives only you might be
sure, because they and you both knew what your reciprocal obligations were as such. The dictates of kinship demanded of relatives that they not harm each
other; so it was necessary first to make relatives of
erstwhile strangers, thus putting them "on the spot,"
and then deal with them on that basis. You assumed
that as relatives they would be trustworthy, and by the
same token you obligated yourself.

But the use of kinship terms of address was only the
beginning, important as it was from the standpoint of
etiquette. The core of the matter was that a proper
mental attitude and a proper conventional behavior

prescribed by kinship must accompany the speaking of each term. As you said "Uncle"—or "Father" or "Brother"—in either address or reference, you must immediately control your thinking of him; you must assume the correct mental attitude due the particular relative addressed, and you must express that attitude in its fitting outward behavior and mien, according to the accepted convention. Thus, term, attitude, behavior, in the correct combinations, were what every member of society must learn and observe undeviatingly. They were standard and inexorable; they had always been. One simply was born into their rule and conformed to them invariably as a matter of course. The more correctly he could do this, whatever the personal sacrifice involved at times, the better member of the group he was, the better his standing as a Dakota, the higher his prestige as a person.

What did this exacting and unrelenting obedience to kinship demands do to the Dakotas? It made them a most kind, unselfish people, always acutely aware of those about them and innately courteous. You see, everyone who would be rated well as a relative had to *make* himself feel and act always in the same way. "How monotonous!" you might say. But it wasn't. For there was as great a variety of permissible attitudes and behaviors as there were kinds of relatives. In that way all the natural human impulses were satisfied: to be gay and irresponsible, or flippant and rude, for fun; to be excessively respectful and dignified; to enjoy being a little foolish, as with those called father and mother; and then to turn serious and protective, as with sons and daughters.

This meant that a socially responsible Dakota might not thoughtlessly indulge his moods, lest there be within range of his voice or presence a kind of relative before whom his feelings must be suppressed as a matter of obligatory respect. He might not be whimsical and unpredictable in his behavior, causing it to be said of him, "He is nice, but I can't ever rely on his being the same way. Now he is charming and polite, and again he is gruff and rude. But that's all right, because I know he means well." If he meant well—that is to say, if he wanted to be known as a good relative— he would not dare act that way. One offense before a respect-relative would be enough!

Now does that sound stuffy and imprisoning? It wasn't one bit. It came natural to a people used to nothing else. It was, in fact, a well oiled, pleasant discipline for group living. To be sure, there were occasional scolds, as among all peoples; but kinship demands tended to keep them down to a minimum, and besides, these persons were considered socially irresponsible and written off as such.

For the most part, then, everyone had his part to play and played it for the sake of his honor, all kinship duties, obligations, privileges, and honorings being reciprocal. One got as well as gave. Thus kinship had everybody in a fast net of interpersonal responsibility and made everybody like it, because its rewards were pleasant. There were fewer rebels against the system than you might think, since, as I have said, social standing and reputation hinged on it. Only those who kept the rules consistently and gladly, thus honoring all their fellows, were good Dakotas—meaning good citizens of society, meaning persons of integrity and reliability. And that was practically all the government there was. It was what men lived by.

Social pressure, always powerful, was particularly strong in such a close-knit group as a camp-circle, where everyone was literally in the public eye. Unless an individual was congenitally perverse or slightly queer he did not care to be aberrant. Indeed, even such a one was likely to be excused and shielded by his relatives, as though he were under an evil spell and could not help it. It was essential that the relatives hold up their end anyway for their own sakes. The failure of one did not excuse another. "Ah, yes, he is like that, has always been . . . still and all, he is my relative," a man might say, and go on playing his own part.

The kinship appeal was always a compelling force in any situation. If two normally decent acquaintances quarreled, for instance—and of course if they were acquaintances they were social relatives—outsiders were deeply concerned over it until it was straightened out. The "good men" felt it incumbent on them to restore peace and order by appealing to the quarreling ones through kinship. Peace is implied by the very name of the people, Odákota, a state or condition of peace; the "O" is a locative prefix.

"We Dakotas love peace within our borders. Peace-making is our heritage. Even as children we settled our little fights through kinship that we might live in Odákota." And with that, two of the most responsible and influential men would visit the unhappy ones and appeal to them to cool off their hearts—for the sake of their relatives who were unhappy over their plight. And they did not go empty-handed. There must always be a token, an outward sign of great inner desire. The peacemakers went prepared to give a gift "to cool off your heart and to show by it that we your kinsmen value your life far above mere chattel."

Such an appeal in kinship's name was supreme. It placed the responsibility for his relatives' peace of mind squarely on the troubled man, reminding him that no Dakota lived unto himself alone; all were bound together in kinship. He might not rightly risk even his very own life needlessly, thereby bringing tears to the eyes of his relatives—especially his sisters and women cousins, to whom he owed the very highest respect and consideration. However slightly he valued himself, he must regard the relatives. And the quarreling men, unable to resist such an appeal, smoked the pipe together and were feasted before the council, and so the breach was healed. Friends, happy over the reconciliation and the restoration of peace, brought them more presents. And it was not in the least the intrinsic value of the gifts that mattered but what they symbolized: that the two were more precious to their relatives than mere things. And thus peace was restored in the camp-circle to the relief of all.

But there was still another situation, even more tense than a quarrel, wherein occasionally the power of kinship rose to its sublime height. The murder of a fellow Dakota was a crime punishable either through immediate reprisal by the kinsmen of the slain or a resort to the ancient ordeals, supervised by the council. I need not describe those ordeals now, except to say that they were almost impossible to survive—humanly speaking. And so, he who did survive was set free, as having been exonerated by a greater than human power—by the Wakan, in fact.

However, now and again, influenced by exceptionally wise leadership, the relatives of a murdered man might agree not to shoot the murderer or demand the ordeal for him, but instead to win his abiding loyalty through kinship. This they did by actually adopting him to be one of them in place of his victim. It was a moving scene when this was done—I wish I could describe it step by step. I have a most impressive account of such an episode, which I transcribed in the Dakota language while old Simon Antelope, a well known, reliable Yankton, told it. I can give only snatches of it here in a free translation:

The angry younger relatives debated the kind of punishment fitting the crime while their wise elder listened, seemingly in accord with them. But after a good while, he began to speak. Skillfully, he began by going along with them:

"My Brothers and Cousins, my Sons and Nephews, we have been caused to weep without shame, men though we are. No wonder we are enraged, for our pride and honor have been grossly violated. Why shouldn't we go out, then, and give the murderer what he deserves?"

Then, after an ominous pause, he suddenly shifted into another gear:

"And yet, my kinsmen, there is a better way!"

Slowly and clearly he explained that better way. They were men of standing, he reminded them, and therefore it was becoming in them to act accordingly. He challenged them to reject the traditional and choose the better way. It was also the hard way, but the only certain way to put out the fire in all their hearts and in the murderer's.

"Each of you bring to me the thing you prize the most. These things shall be a token of our intention. We shall give them to the murderer who has hurt us, and he shall thereby become 'something to us' [an idiom for relative] in place of him who is gone. Was the dead your brother? Then this man shall be your brother. Or your uncle? Or your cousin? As for me, he was my nephew; and so this man shall be my nephew. And from now on, he shall be one of us, and our endless concern shall be to regard him as though he were truly our loved one come back to us."

And they did just that. The slayer was brought to the council not knowing what his fate was to be. Steeling himself for the worst, he kept his eyes averted. He did not try to infer the decision by peering into the councilmen's faces. He was not going to have it said of him in after years, "Poor thing! How I pitied him! Like some hunted creature, he tried furtively to read mercy in men's eyes!" No, he would not flinch at having to give up his life after taking another's. He too was a man!

But when the council's speaker offered him the peace pipe saying, "Smoke now with these your new relatives, for they have chosen to take you to themselves in place of one who is not here," his heart began to melt.

"It is their heart's wish that henceforth you shall be one of them; shall go out and come in without fear. Be confident that their love and compassion which were his are now yours forever!" And, during that speech, tears trickled down the murderer's face.

"He had been trapped by loving kinship," my informant said, "and you can be sure that he made an even better relative than many who are related by blood, because he had been bought at such a price." And what might easily have become burning rancor and hatred, perhaps leading to further violence, was purged away from the hearts of all.

It was, of course, obligatory on all the slain man's immediate relatives by blood and marriage to receive him properly. And the men, women, and even children quickly fell into line, without awkwardness, accepting the situation and behaving according as each was now related to him. Those proper attitudes and behaviors accompanying each term were, as I have said before, ingrained in them from constant practice until they

were automatic. Until they were instinctive, I nearly
said, but of course that is not the word. It is not instinctive to be unselfish, kind, and sincere toward
others, and therefore courteous. Those are traits that
have to be learned. And they can be learned, but only
by scrupulous repetition, until they become automatic
responses; until, in the case of the Dakotas, the very
uttering of a kinship term at once brought the whole
process into synchronic play—kinship term, attitude,
behavior—like a chord that is harmonious.

To summarize, and perhaps also to catch up some
points not yet clear, I have this to say:

This chapter tries to give the basic principles of the
Dakota kinship system and to explain its purpose and
influence in tribal life. What I have given here is, of
course, the ideal picture. But I can honestly say that
hardly one in a hundred dared to be thought of as
deviating from its rule, although there were always a
few naturally heedless persons who persistently or occasionally disregarded it. But that at once classed them
with the *witko*—the naughty, irresponsible child, the
outlaw adult, the mentally foolish, the drunk. No
adult in his right mind cared to be so classed.

I run a risk in leaving this subject with such an
emphasis on the facility with which new relatives could
be made. I don't mean that a Dakota could not rest
until he had feverishly gone round the entire camp-
circle establishing relationships. After all, the sphere
of kith and kin is limited for even a Dakota. When I
say that kinship was all-inclusive and co-extensive with

the tribe, I mean it was that potentially. It was true that everyone was related to all the people within his own circle of acquaintances. But all those people also had other circles of acquaintance within the large tribe. All such circles overlapped and interlocked. Any Dakota could legitimately find his way to any other, if he wished or needed to do so. And thus, with relatives scattered over the many camp-circles and communities, anyone could go visiting anywhere, and be at home.

Perhaps now it can be better realized how, for publicity purposes, almost any Sioux entertainer can quite blandly claim to be a grandson of Sitting Bull. He probably is!

5: LIFE IN TIPI AND CAMP-CIRCLE

FOR THE DAKOTA FAMILY OF SOMETHING MORE THAN a century ago "home" was a conical dwelling made by stretching a skin tent over a framework of poles. The self-respecting family's tipi, far from being an impromptu affair, was constructed according to rule and erected with care so that it would look right as well as withstand the rigors of weather. Women erected the tipi, unless it was an oversized chief's lodge or the council-tipi, in which case men raised the long, heavy poles.

Each family set up its tipi in such a way as to help form the camp-circle, the unifying ring of which they were all a vital part. All tipis faced the council-tipi, which stood in the center of the great open common and was the focus of community life and thought. It was a town hall of sorts. The four magistrates lived there during their term of office. But they were not the whole law, except during migrations and communal buffalo hunts when they planned the movements of the group and called on one of the soldier societies to carry out their orders. That whole setup is interesting, but it is not pertinent here, except to say that this active dictatorship lasted only during times of mass action, when it was required for the common good.

The council-tipi was a lively place. Men came and went, and nobody was barred from it. The men of mature judgment came to deliberate and plan and philosophize; and the little men of no particular standing, quiet souls who harmlessly lived out their ineffectual lives—they are in every race—came and sat along the fringes to listen in and to eat.

The women by turns honored their men by taking cooked food, the best they had, to the council-tipi. Directly it was taken from them, they hurried away. But don't assume that they were chased off. They left because it was considered unwomanly to push one's way into a gathering of the other sex; it was unmanly for men to do so under opposite circumstances. Outsiders seeing women keep to themselves have frequently expressed a snap judgment that they were regarded as inferior to the noble. male. The simple fact is that woman had her own place and man his; they were not the same and neither inferior nor superior.

The sharing of work also was according to sex. Both had to work hard, for their life made severe demands. But neither expected the other to come and help outside the customary division of duties; each sex thought the other had enough to do. That did not mean, however, that a man disdained to do woman's work when necessary; or a woman, man's. The attitude on division of work was quite normal, however it looked to outsiders. A woman caring for children and doing all the work around the home thought herself no worse off than her husband who was compelled to risk his life continuously, hunting and remaining ever on guard against enemy attacks on his family.

But to get back to the tipi. I said it was home to the family. But the father-mother-child unit was not final and isolated; it was only one of several others forming the larger family, the *tiyośpaye* (tee-yo'-shpah-yay). This Dakota word is essential in describing tribal life. It denotes a group of families, bound together by blood and marriage ties, that lived side by side in the camp-circle. There was perfect freedom of movement. Any family for reasons valid to itself could depart at any time to visit relatives or sojourn for longer or shorter periods in some other Dakota camp-circle. There was no power to hold them back.

Those camp-circles were peripatetic villages, periodically on the move over the vast Dakota domain. They were ever in search of food, going seasonally where deer-hunting was good or where certain fruits of the earth were abundant and ready for gathering. Occasionally two camp-circles met up by chance and camped together awhile, convivially. And for annual celebrations several of them came together by prearrangement, and made one immense circle.

All the families of a *tiyośpaye* operated as a single unit in practically all activities. Men often hunted in company; women did their work, especially fancywork, in pleasant circles; the *tiyośpaye* horses were kept in a common herd off on some grassy spot, tended by the youth under adult supervision. Every two or three families used the same outdoor cooking fire; and any woman was happy and ready to include in her family circle whoever happened by. It was that informal, harmonious, and natural, since they were all closely related. Whenever a child was born or someone died, or if one of the members was undergoing a special ceremony, the inevitable gift-giving was the kinship obligation and privilege of as many as could cooperate to make it a creditable affair.

But while it was true that the *tiyośpaye* operated as one in ceremonies and feasts, in getting food, or accomplishing needed tasks for the common good, and while all meat was freely shared and liberally dispensed, the Dakota people were not communistic in the sense that everything belonged to all and nothing belonged exclusively to one. Goods were not pooled to be shared alike. It was true, instead, that as long as something was in a person's possession, it was his sole right to give or withhold it; there was no individual or agency with authority to compel his surrendering it against his wishes. Kinship alone could do just that, impelling him. It made him ready and happy at all times to give up *anything* whenever a situation developed challenging him to rise to his full stature as a relative.

Not only in their material life did the related families function as a unit. The members did so even more in spirit in all their interacting relationships. A woman who had to leave her children behind to go on a journey went with an easy conscience. She knew that her several "sisters" and the rest would never let a child be abused or allowed to stray off or go hungry. When she stayed home and other mothers went, it was the same. It was not even necessary to exact definite promises, "Will you be sure to keep an eye on my child?" To say that would be to doubt the other's sense of kinship responsibility, and that would be an insult. Of course she would; why ask?

As for the child, you can see what it did for him to have so many persons responsible for him. It gave him multiple protection. It insured for him the care that is due all helpless children, even when their own parents might not be there. It was a very comfortable and safe feeling for a growing child. Moreover, it was a great advantage for him to have many contacts with different persons so early, and continually have to adjust to them. His circle was never limited; he was used to society from the start. There never was that moment in his life when he was suddenly faced with the bewilderment of having to adjust to many strangers at once after a life shielded from people. He was born not into a secluded single family, but into a *tiyośpaye.*

If I have said this often before, I say it again: every child must remember to use the proper kinship term for each person, and feel properly toward him, and behave in the conventionally correct way, all simultaneously. This preoccupation with such duties deflected a child's attention from himself, preventing his becoming unduly self-conscious. From the necessity for constant regard toward others, he derived a certain emotional stability and poise in talking to adults. Even in a small child it seemed that the spoken kinship terms made him instantly thoughtful and responsible.

Nor was it any wonder that small children rapidly learned their social duties, since the training constantly given them was calculated to condition them and direct them in that way. All grownups by tacit consent seemed to "gang up" for this purpose. Even before a child was aware of his kinship obligations, they made sentences and put the correct words and formal speeches into his mouth for him to repeat to this or that relative. It was their informal but constant system of education in human relations and social responsibility.

There are vestiges of this training still going on among the more remotely situated Dakotas. Not so long ago, I observed the following incident, which illustrates what I am saying.

A woman had been guarding a newborn grandchild asleep in a blanket on the ground. But now she had to leave. So she called her own little five-year-old boy from his play and said to him, *"Cinkś* [Son], stay here until I come back and take care of him. He is your little son, so do not leave him alone." She spoke earnestly as if to an adult, an equal, avoiding baby talk. "See that he is not stepped on, he is so tiny—and scare the flies for him."

When I saw him later on he was still on the job. Truly "a picket frozen on duty." Wistfully his eyes followed his playmates near by, merry and noisy, but he stuck to his post. Already he knew that a father does not desert his son. He was still "scaring flies," by crooking a small arm and moving it from side to side a trifle above the infant's face, desultorily enough, to be sure, but faithfully.

I have been talking so far mostly about the corporate life of the *tiyospaye*. Now for a look at the family life within one of the tipis.

In its way, life was well organized there, with a definite place for everybody. The members of the family had their own spaces where they habitually sat, ate, slept, and worked. Everyone kept his personal things in skin containers, which were always ornamented, sometimes handsomely. These were secured only as far as tying strings could make them so. There were no locks and keys, but they were not missed. A good relative did not open another's things. Even small children were gently but firmly warned to leave things alone.

Grandmothers were especially zealous in admonishing the children because they had little else to do. "Do not touch that, Grandchild! It is theirs. [Impersonal.] See, nobody does so." This meant "You must not either." There was something in Dakota upbringing that made children amazingly docile and tractable. The standard words "See, nobody does so" were effective most of the time.

If you looked into such a tipi of the past as I am talking about, you might see only the surface untidiness—the unavoidable dirt, discomfort, and inconvenience incident to primitive life lived on the ground. Those would be the obvious features, and you might come away thinking that was all. And that would be a pity, for underneath that surface lay something very wonderful—the spiritual life of a patient, unselfish, and courteous people who disciplined themselves without letup to keep the tribal ideal at all costs.

It was this respect for personality that ruled tipi life and made it tolerable for the several, and sometimes many, who dwelt there. Outsiders, accustomed to many rooms, would be justified in asking, "How could anybody know privacy here? How could a man think his own thoughts, packed in with so many?" And those would be good questions for which there are good answers.

The Dakotas managed to achieve privacy in their own adroit fashion. They made their own privacy, and it was mentally effected. Harmonious tipi life was easily possible by each person's knowing and playing his rôle well. He moved cautiously at all times, with a nice regard for the rights of others, according to his relationship to each.

Whenever the tipi was erected for a long stay, as in

winter quarters, back rests were set up, marking off each person's tiny compartment. But beyond these material barriers, there was that sense of decency and honor, inbred as part of kinship obligation, that kept the eyes on things rather than on people. Dakotas did not have to stare intently into the face of a speaker in order to understand him. They kept the head down or looked into space while they listened politely, attending with the mind alone. They do that to this day. And in the tipi they were extra careful. No one who cared for his standing wanted to be so much as suspected of looking about askance to see what he could so easily see if he tried.

As for thinking one's thoughts in a crowded tipi, it was more possible to those accustomed to it than you might think. All tipi conversation was normally geared low for that purpose, with little excitement evident in the voice. The attitude of a speaker in a group was generally not indicated so much by exclamatory outbursts and other variations of tone as by idiom. Thus anyone could withdraw from the group in spirit and think undisturbed, even with talking going on all about him.

This does not mean that there never was a hilarious hour in a tipi. Occasionally there was, but only when it was planned—when the company was a select one, composed of the kinds of relatives who were not under the compulsion of dignified behavior toward one another. Groups of fathers and sons, or brothers-in-law who were in joking relationship, or brothers and male cousins, would be examples. But the presence of any who were in the "avoidance" or "respect" relationship had a moderating effect, for part of their duty was to control themselves, in mutual deference.

I must say a word about the children. If the adults sat around the central fire for a social hour, the children grouped off to one side to carry on there in a whispered good time. They could indulge in gay, unvoiced laughter, so as not to disturb the adults, and be perfectly happy. They might appear to be restricted and relegated to one side to be got out of the way; actually they preferred to be there and to have their fun in their own quiet way. This controlled manner was definitely their pattern of behavior in public. But when they were off somewhere, with only their own kind, the children were far from quiet. They could cut loose then and be as merry and noisy as any other children.

Every caller was immediately offered courtesy food. Sometimes it was very little, but it was there—unless of course there was no more food on hand anywhere. Food had to be graciously accepted, even if the caller had just eaten elsewhere. What he could not consume he carried away as *wateca* to be eaten later. And it was proper to return the dish to the hostess with a certain phrase that was conventional. A person who neglected to return his dish or who failed to murmur the right words of thanks was considered ill-bred. That was the universal custom of hospitality. It was, as I have already said, the great tribal ideal, so automatically practised that the admonitions of certain elderly men

and women who were given to haranguing the young
seemed hardly necessary:

"Give food! Give food unstintingly! Let nothing be
held in reserve for one alone. When all food is gone,
then we shall honorably starve together. Let us still be
Dakotas!"

In the minds of the people, the logical reactions to
such undue advice would be: "Of course! Certainly,
those are true words. But why bring them up? If we
did not give food, just what would be left for us to do?
What else could we become if we did not remain Dakotas?" The two things—being hospitable and being
Dakotas—were mystically one; to try to omit either
was to destroy the whole, and that was unthinkable.

In this chapter I have discussed informally many
things that blend and overlap and so cannot be separated under any rigid scheme of treatment. But certain points may be restated here for further emphasis:

The family unit of parents-and-child was not the
final and complete idea it is elsewhere. It was an integral part of the larger family, the *tiyospaye*, bound
together with blood and marriage ties. The individuals
constituting these larger groups bore definite relationships to each other and owed one another definite duties. They functioned as a unit, materially and spiritually, in a never-ending interplay of honorings one to
another, young and old.

First the Dakota said, "Be a good relative. That is
of paramount importance!" And then, "Be related,

somehow, to everyone you know; make him important to you; he also is a man." This was done, you remember, by the careful establishing of all valid kinship, whether through blood or affinity. But then, seeing that some people were still left out, formal relationships with them were manufactured through a social kinship system—an ingenious method for including everyone in the great Ring of Relatives.

Then the Dakota said, "Be generous!" (How unnecessary! Would anyone withhold that which is good from his very own?) "Be hospitable!" (Why not? Should a man eat while his brother starves?)

With such unuttered reasoning, the Dakotas fitted every detail of existence together, as into a neat mosaic, to make their own peculiar "scheme of life that worked."

6: PRAYING FOR POWER

WHERE NO RECORDS EXIST THERE CAN BE NO FINAL and absolute treatment of a phase of Indian life as it flourished well over a hundred years ago. The Dakota people of the past were not asked to analyze for posterity their beliefs about God. We cannot really know, therefore, in so many words by them uttered, exactly what they believed and how they expressed that belief. We can only get it from stories that have come down. Even the oldest informant today is far too young.

Personally, I have never had a chance to question any but Christian Dakotas, except for one man who, though baptized, preferred to practise his religion in the pagan manner—meaning pagan as the opposite of Christian and without any derogatory overtones. Yet even he had been born into a society already influenced, undeniably, by Christianity and he was not hostile to the church. Perhaps he was eighty, he thought he was, yet he was amazingly keen and alert, and he was physically youthful in his lightness, speed, and agility. He was an Indian ascetic, if I ever saw one, lean and clear-eyed. He made a most reliable informant about the ancient religious practices of his people.

As for the others, they were all men mature in their Christianity, men of integrity, known to all the people as leaders of thought, and influential in personal example. Two of them were clergymen. Completely at home and active in their church life, they yearned for no outgrown and ancient way. Even so, without exception they talked about the belief of their forefathers with a tender reverence that was beautiful. Obviously it was not for them; yet neither was it therefore something to treat lightly, to be amused at, or to conceal with shame. Quite simply they discussed the subject without questioning even those things about it that are incredible today, because it was their grandfathers who once believed it and told them so. There are some things you do not try to rationalize; you just accept with bowed head: the Wisemen following a Star; the Shepherds who heard the *Gloria in Excelsis;* the Resurrection and Glorious Ascension. These informants talked about the religion of their ancestors in that spirit. So shall we look at it here. Who am I to question what was once very real and solemn to others?

But first of all we must know something of the terms they used. The basic Dakota word in this area is *wakan*. God is Wakan. By whatever name a people may call him, he is still the same. I mean that Almighty Power, invisible, but nonetheless real, even to the most primitive. They feel there is a Power greater than themselves, which in all ages and all climes they strive somehow to understand. The Dakotas called him by various terms: Wakan (Holy, Mysterious, Magical, Inscrutable); Taku-Wakan (Something-Holy); Taku-Skanskan (Something-in-Movement); Wakantanka (Great Holy—commonly translated as the Great Spirit); and, finally, Wahupa, an untranslatable term in the sacred language of the esoteric.

Of course, it cannot be said of any race that every single member of it is occupied with religious speculation and aspiration to the exclusion of all other subjects. Nevertheless, it was a Dakota trait to be religious, always subconsciously aware of the Supernatural Power. Before it, they felt helpless and humble. It was not smart to try to conquer that Power, or to defy or blaspheme it. They did not speak flippantly of it while they were safe and gay, and then have to turn about and run right back to it when they were frightened. That was unsportsmanlike; it was undignified, too. And if your Dakota wanted to be any one thing,

it was to be dignified at all times. The people were
imbued with some age-old wisdom that said all men
must bow to the Wakan, anyway, so it is best to stay
bowed and not have to bow perforce.

Though I talked with them at different times, and
individually for the most part, my informants all felt
that it was an error to say the Dakotas actually wor-
shipped rocks, trees, the four winds, and other mani-
festations of nature. "They are not themselves Wakan,
but the Wakan is in all things. When our people wished
to pray, they selected some common tree or rock, un-
touched by man, and set it apart for its sacred use by
painting it red. And then they addressed it, for now
it was Wakan." One man so explained it. From this
it would appear that the Dakotas do not believe their
ancestors prayed to a common tree or a rock. I am not
saying; for I do not know. From certain ancient
prayer-songs, it does seem clear that the one praying
spoke not to the Wakan, but to the rock or the tree.
And yet—and this is important—it is not the common
everyday name for rock or tree that is used, but, instead, archaic words, belonging exclusively to an ancient "sacred language," *tunkan* for rock, and *paza* for
tree. That word *tunkan* is a generic that seems to indicate eternity—"ancient of days." It is also inherent
in the term for all ancestors from the second ascending
generation, the grandfather, and going back endlessly.
Agelessness, eternity, a staying quality, are suggested
by *tunkan*. It has parallels in Christian terminology,
such as "Rock of Ages."

One never hears *paza* today, except perhaps in some fragment of song or legend. It suggests the idea of uprightness, because a tree is perpendicular instead of horizontal. It is active, alive. It is not supine, passive, dead. Make of that what you will; I can only define the word.

The Dakotas really feared one medium of the Wakan, "the thunders," because they were so whimsical and unpredictable. You could not tell where they would strike. It seemed as if they enjoyed playing tricks on the people. They had to be placated in a peculiar way. All other forms of *wakan* revelation—a flowing river, a growing plant, the warming sun, and even fire—were benevolent and reliable. If any one of these did harm, like flood or fire, it was man's own fault for not doing his part. You could not hold that against them. But the thunders! What their program was, how they operated, it was impossible to know. If they had a plan at all, men could not figure it out. They were special, unique, foolish. They had to be appealed to in kind. And so, praying to the thunders was the one and only time when the Dakotas dropped their normal dignity, much against their nature, and literally made fools of themselves, to be laughed at by all the people.

At these times they enacted what was called the Heyoka-Wozepi, fantastic, comical, tragic ceremony, wherein everything was done opposite to meaning. The more earnestly the participants prayed, the more they behaved like clowns, fanning themselves in the cold or shivering in the summer sun, putting up an awning with meticulous detail, and then sitting on the sunny side of it, and all that kind of thing. I can't describe it in detail here. I can only assure you that this was the one instance when the Wakan was feared, really actively feared. "The thunders are *wicaśaśni* [not men, because deceptive]; you cannot treat with them as men."

But the unhappy clowns who enacted these silly rôles were doing it out of dire necessity. They did it because they had had a dream in which they saw the Heyoka, the manlike messenger of the thunders, and their own selves doing incredibly ridiculous things together. They, little helpless men, must imitate the messenger's antics publicly out of fear of his wrath if they refused. Sometimes what they did in their dreams was grotesque and cruelly undignified, but they had to enact the parts faithfully, on pain of death. And who would kill them, if they ignored that dream? Why, the thunders of course. So they hastened to carry out the dream before all the people. Fortunately these Heyoka dreams did not come often or to any great number of people. It was in daytime naps that the Heyoka dreams were likely to come; so such naps were avoided as much as possible. When one had such a dream, it was truly a calamity. If a thunder storm came up before all the arrangements were made for the ceremony—for some dreams were very complicated and required much preparation—then not only the victim but his terrified relatives wailed pitiably as the storm approached, and waited momentarily for the lightning to strike. It was perhaps the saddest bondage to the Inscrutable that the people knew.

As I have said, most other prayers were more rational, made to a rational medium of Wakan that could be counted on to answer with due respect, honor, and dignity as a man to his relative. The river was always implored as the giver of beauty. The four winds and the earth and the sun were all benevolent mediums.

The prayers to the sun were the most ardent of all. In the annual sun dance, which lasted many days, everything was done in decency and order. Time was taken for it. There was no hurry because this was the whole of life. Nothing was so important as that those men who had cried out to God in their distress during the year should offer themselves here, votive offerings in fulfillment of their pledge. This was the great corporate prayer, the highlight of Dakota life. So the people followed in droves to wherever the next of many successive preliminary rites was to take place. They attended the ceremonial setting up of the sun dance booth. They watched the "man of gentle speech" as he dug the hole where the sacred pole, as a symbol of life, would stand in the center of the dance, and then as he buried at its base certain requisite gifts. He had been chosen out of honor. Every task assigned was an honor and given to the worthy. There was no buying one's way in.

The people even went out to the woods to look on while the "scouts" indulged in dramatics, thereby locating the tree from which the pole would be fashioned

and taking it in a surprise attack. They watched the
beautiful little rite, "Apology to the Birds"—an apology for taking their tree, their home. Then they saw
the eight "beloveds," whose families had arranged for
them to cut the sacred pole—symbolically, of course,
simply touching the ax to it. Afterward feasts would
be given in their honor that all men might eat once
again.

Bringing the felled tree home was a sight. It rested
on crosspoles, reverently carried by men, much like
pallbearers. In the meantime, all the people who went
out-decked themselves in green boughs from the trees,
each one aiming to include at least one twig from the
trimmings of the sacred tree, to be worn for its benefi-
cent effect. And when they started back toward the
camp-circle they made a veritable moving forest. Talk
about Birnam wood! The effect was the same. Riders
made festoons of leaves to decorate their horses and
hung huge green collars about their necks and gar-
lands about their legs. And they made great shields
for themselves and wound wreaths around their heads.
It was most beautiful and impressive. When they were
within running distance from camp, they all dashed
homeward in a sham raid—thrilling and a little frightening to watch. (When I was a child, I saw a re-enact-
ment of such a raid at Fort Yates, North Dakota. I
have never lost the picture. It was pageantry in the
raw!)

The dance itself was terribly moving. Men carried
out in exact detail the vows that they had made to the

Wakan: that they would give one hundred pieces of their living flesh, or would pierce their chest or back muscles with skewers and attach themselves by ropes to the sacred pole and dance so. It was a bloody and tearful sight. Not that the victims wept, but their respect-relatives—their sisters and cousins—and their mothers and aunts and grandmothers did so. It must be understood that all suffering was self-dictated and self-imposed. No man ever told another how he should scarify and torture himself in order to pray; nor yet that he should desist, once he had made a promise to God.

The climax came just before dawn, the last dawn after a vigil of forty-eight hours or more, when finally the dancers could properly stop and were led staggering away to rest on their sagebrush couches. Then the holy man, the leader, came to the pole and clasped it tightly with both arms, letting the rest of his body hang inert as with emotions unutterable he wailed ceremonially in behalf of all the people. His rôle was to wail an entreaty to the Wakan through the sun. He wailed importunately, like a child insisting on a favor; he wailed that all the hopes and desires and all the private prayers of all hearts might be realized.

It was an unspeakably holy moment, the holiest in the life of these people. It touched them deeply, for it had to do with their very existence. Some who had desperate needs—a dying child to be restored, and so on—wept softly. When the wailing man had finished he seated himself by the buffalo-skull altar at the base of the pole, fixed his eyes on the eastern sky, and waited.

And the people also turned to watch, all in awesome
silence. Then, presently, after a colorful promise, there
was the sun once again! Dazzling, powerful, unfailing
—no wonder the Dakotas thought it holy! It was. And
it was so personal, too. Quickly it sought them all out,
great or small, and warmed each one most pleasantly
and individually at the one instant, impartially. Everyone sighed with satisfaction. Avoiding common talk,
they dispersed in all directions toward their tipis for
another year, confident that ill would skirt their borders because they had done their part beautifully and
well.

I still have to explain another phase of Dakota religious life, the quest for a vision. In contrast to that
one corporate religious expression, the sun dance, all
other experience of prayer was private and solitary.
It is said by some that originally this was the only way
until the custom grew up of joining together in the fulfillment of vows by all those who had pledged themselves during the year. This that I shall describe now
is perhaps the oldest, antedating the horse age. Mystics
are lonely. Among all peoples they reach out ahead of
the masses, and here too that was true. "Lonely is the
man with vision." Only certain individuals felt in-
escapably the call for this effort. By the time a man
reached his latter teens he might begin to feel restless
and to want some definite influence to guide his future.
Such a man decided to fast. So he whispered his idea
to some relative, usually a man cousin who himself had
gone through a like experience in his youth. The rela-

tive helped the novice to prepare. Absolute mastery of physical desires was the prerequisite. The candidate underwent a powerful cleansing through the sweat bath and remained apart after that. Meantime, his "altar," at a place of his own choosing, was prepared for him by his relative.

Then, quietly at some hour unannounced and without fanfare, the young man and his companion slipped away. At the altar, usually on the edge of a remote butte, the man took his place, there to remain all alone on the hallowed plot until someone came to lead him into the *wakan* realm. There he hoped to see something supernaturally significant that would help him become a worth-while man: a good hunter, a good warrior, an effective and true medicine man, a diviner, or whatever. He wanted power to be useful in his tribe.

He ate and drank nothing; he had only his pipe. After he had fasted a long time, having begun at home of course, his head became light and his senses became so delicate and acute that even a little bit of stick pricking him was unbearably intensified. If a bird called, he might hear a message from the spirit world. If an animal approached him, he might see it as a man to guide him to his vision. Thus he might have the experience of being led by that "man" through the air or over land and sea, resting at last at some spot not to be found on earth where he would receive his revelation. If he heard a song there, he brought it back; if he saw animals or men being restored to life by eating certain herbs, he took careful note of them. In such a

case it was his function in life to become a healer and
these would be the medicines he would use.

I cannot give any one fasting experience in detail
here. They were all very holy, and they were all very
involved. They were remembered with photographic
clarity, and took a very long while to tell. I have secured several such narratives. They follow the same
general pattern, yet in detail they are as varied as
human imagination is varied.

Dakota religious life was purely individual. There
was nothing that all must do with reference to God, but
only what each man felt as an inner compulsion that
could not be denied. Not every Dakota sought a vision;
the majority did not, and nobody criticized another
for that. It was entirely a matter of individual decision.

A man who had gone through such a spiritual experience would ever after hold in reverence the animal
whose spirit led him and would feel a kinship with it.
Whenever he was in need of supernatural help he could
become *en rapport* with that spirit and was thereby
suddenly enabled to do what was humanly impossible.
He was no longer a plain man but one imbued with
supernatural strength and power. To get *en rapport*
the visionary sometimes merely thought on his mentor
and reached him in that way; at other times he "demonstrated" him by publicly acting out the rôle of that
animal in some characteristic way. While in that rôle
he was mystically identified with it, and through it he
derived the superhuman power needed for some special

crisis. He thus brought before that mentor of his their spiritual brotherhood and so became *re*-related to him. As much as to say, "Remember me? I am he to whom you made that promise. Now I need its fulfillment." And such a man earnestly believed he would get that power, and so he did.

This act of reminding a spiritual brother and calling on his help was spoken of as "Remembering oneself as bear"—or eagle, or whatever. I can't do better than illustrate.

A warrior was so badly hurt that he could not take a step. But when his enemies came back a few days later and he had to get away or be killed, this is what the narrative reports: "He slashed a rabbit skin in two strips, tied them about his shattered ankles, and so, 'remembering himself as rabbit,' he ran leaping and bounding away, nor did he feel the hurt any more." To the initiated this would mean that here was a man whose mentor was the rabbit-spirit.

A closing word about the buffalo. We say, "The buffalo was the Dakotas' god." Well, it depends on what is meant by that word "god." At any rate, he was the Dakotas' guardian, their arch-relative, who cared most for their physical sustenance. According to legend, a Dakota found his way by chance into the underworld where the buffalo nation lived, and there, with bow and arrow, was able to rid them of a perpetual menace. In gratitude the buffalo-chiefs promised to follow him and his offspring forever. "As long as we live, you too shall live and shall prosper." That sounded like "for all time." No wonder, then, that when the buffalo were killed off wantonly, within a few years' time after the white men came, the Dakotas almost lost their lives, too.

Indeed the buffalo was everything to the Dakotas' well-being: food, shelter, fuel, toys, implements, clothing, and much more. His was, therefore, the chief of all spirits serving as mediums for deriving supernatural good. But, whereas all the others were personal and private mediums for certain individuals according to their fasting and vision, the buffalo by covenant belonged to all. So of course everybody revered him. He was the embodiment of sacrifice that others might live. He came when they were starving; he set them the example of hospitality; he was host to a whole nation.

Before closing, I want to add that, originally, and while these practices were going strong, vision experiences were never divulged to just anybody. One who made his revelation common by relating it in a secular fashion was regarded as not being truthful, as inventing a tale. The proper procedure was for the visionary upon his return and after his second purification to report his vision only to such as had also had like experiences—old men who had lived their lives according to the guidance received supernaturally in a vision.

Action, all in a minute, through inspiration; artistic ability, not acquired with repetitious practice but learned in the mind only and then suddenly brought to light—these were further religious ideas of the past. I wish there were space to explain them.

7: EDUCATION—BY PRECEPT AND EXAMPLE

IN PREVIOUS CHAPTERS I HAVE ALREADY SPOKEN OF things that most appropriately belong here. I could not avoid doing so. All life, all the culture of a people, is of a piece. No element of it exists in a vacuum. I have already described informal education through kinship observances. What we might call the formal education of Dakota youth was centered in the tribal ceremonies. The "sermons" recited on these occasions emphasized the ideals that each generation felt it vital to implant in the minds of its boys and girls. Let us look at several of these ceremonies to see what teaching accompanied them.[1]

We may begin with the Hunka ceremony performed on the happy occasion of blessing little children. The small candidate was honored by a feast and presents were made to many people in his or her name. The recipients asked singers to laud the child's name in song; and all that was very agreeable. But the core of the whole matter was that, by the child's very presence as the center of attention and acclaim, he or she was henceforth a "child-beloved," and was committed as a matter of honor to the practice of generosity, even

[1] The ceremonial speeches quoted in this chapter were recorded by Miwakan-Yuha (George Sword) in the Dakota language many years ago; translated by Ella Deloria in 1939 for the Bureau of American Ethnology.

if at times it might involve great personal sacrifice.

I have heard an elderly woman or man say, "I gave that person my last food, remembering I am a *hunka.*" It was a kind of *noblesse oblige,* forever compelling them.

The candidates—usually several were entered for this rite by their respective families, who shared in the giving and the feast—sat in a row, each one holding a beautiful blue ear of corn mounted on a stick, symbol of food ever growing and of fecundity. When the officiant was ready to deliver the sermon, he took a braided strip of sweet grass, dipped its purposely frayed ends into water, and made as if to touch each child's extended tongue. But then he withdrew it, saying:

"The children-beloved of all time now add you to their ranks. As you go on from here, there may be those near you who are faint and weak. Of such you shall ever be mindful. Though you would hastily bring water to your own lips to quench your thirst, yet you shall pause and look about you first—behind you and before you and from side to side."

And only then he let each child taste the water.

Next he threw sweet grass and tobacco and other herbs and leaves on the fire, smothering the flame until it gave forth a smudge highly aromatic. Then he cut a small bit of buffalo tongue, cooked and lying ready, and held it over the fire, letting the incense play over it thoroughly. Cutting the meat into two exact parts, and laying one piece on the child's tongue while he cast the other symbolically into the fire, he said:

"Wherever you sit down to eat, there may perhaps
be someone waiting near, hungry for a swallow of your
food. At such a time, you shall remember what you are
[a *hunka*]. And though you were even then lifting meat
to your mouth, yet you shall stop midway. You shall
forbear to eat it all alone. But only what might fill
one cheek, that you shall eat. And with the rest, you
shall show mercy."

Thus were the small children, at psychologically the
right moment, made to accept the idea of personal responsibility for the wants of others.

Hospitality was again brought forcibly home to
young girls in the Ghost Feast. For example, when
four granddaughters of a once prominent and popular
woman, famous for hospitality, were honor guests at
her Ghost Feast this is what happened. The officiant
incensed some pemmican—the sacrificial element—and
placed a bit of it on each girl's tongue, saying, as for
the ghost:

"This food I deliver to you. This food, mixed with
perfume leaf and redolent with incense, you shall hold
in your mouth, while you realize that in future no matter who enters your tipi to sit him down . . . he shall
be your concern, and for him you shall break in two
that which you might have eaten alone. So shall you
share."

The Ghost Feast was nicely calculated to touch the
impressionable adolescent girl and it did exactly that.
Overcome by the wailing of their elders and the solem-
nity of the officiant's moving words, which seemed to

issue from the ghost-bundle like a last admonition from their dear kind grandmother, it did seem to the girls that nothing could ever be more important than the continuance of her spirit of hospitality. And now her mantle was falling upon them. Should her good deeds die with her? Never, if they could help it!

The Dakotas firmly believed that what a person felt, thought, and did during some emotional crisis in life, became a habit supernaturally operating, almost like a spell, from which he could hardly change. Times of grief were such times. The period of a girl's passing into womanhood was for her definitely such a time. It was then that the ideals of purity and chastity and of true wifehood and noble motherhood were especially stressed by means of the Buffalo Ceremony, in which the girl on whose account it was performed was the sole and central character. It was too intricate and parabolic a ceremony to explain here. Let me just quote the formal teaching words the officiant recited in her presence:

"A real woman is virtuous and soft-spoken and modest and does not shame her husband and neglect her children. She is skillful in the womanly arts and hospitable to all who enter her dwelling. She remains at home ready to receive guests at all times. Her fire burns permanently cheery and smoke curls prettily upward from her tipi-head."

At this ceremony, the girl's "respect-relations," her brothers and cousins, gave generously in her name. Later on, if, forgetting a little her obligation, she in-

clined to run around with careless girls whose parents
either had not cared or could not afford the ceremony
for them, her mothers and grandmothers reminded her
—through kinship again!—saying:

"Your brothers and cousins gave away many fine
horses in your honor. Can it be that they acted so nobly
all in vain?" That was enough for a thoughtful girl.
Long before, she had learned the relationship between
opposite sexes of the same generation—that they must
respect each other's feelings with full reciprocity. So
she must not shame her brothers and cousins by getting a bad reputation. That fact was a check on her at
such times.

Boys had their lessons as well. Besides participating
in the Hunka ceremony and being made "children-
beloved" by it, they were trained in every way to be
daring and brave and to endure hardship without cry-
ing out. And if a precocious boy sneaked away and
joined a war party, the warriors put him through certain tests of courage that were hard, not to say danger-
ous. If he passed them, he was one up on the boys who
stayed behind. He brought back certain awards, one
to show he had passed the danger tests, and the other
to show he had done successful scouting—though perhaps he had seen only the tracks of a deer near a
waterhole. No boy could very well be subject to abuse
on a war party, because it was sure to include relatives.
They of course owed him obligatory duties, even under
the unusual circumstances.

Thus Dakota education was promoted: informally,

through their ceaseless practice in human relations within the kinship circle; formally, in the teachings of the ceremonies, as well as in legends. Manual education—how to do this or do that—was the least of it. That simply came in the doing. Children were generally not given menial tasks to discourage them at the outset. They were given new materials to start on, so as to sustain their interest. Normal skill thus came in the actual doing. The mothers generally did the cooking and other work around the tipi, while the grandmothers, as long as they were physically able, provided fuel and water. It was all part of a pattern. However it might seem from the outside, the grandmothers wanted to do that, so as not to make life irksome for children at the start—just as their grandmothers had spared them. Each in her own turn.

8: ECONOMICS: GIVING TO HAVE

GIVING WAS GLORIFIED. THE FORMAL "GIVE-AWAY" was a bonafide Dakota institution. Naturally it followed that things changed hands with readiness when the occasion demanded, since the best teaching said things were less important than people; that pride lay in honoring relatives rather than in amassing goods for oneself; that a man who failed to participate in the giving customs was a suspicious character, something less than a human being.

If someone made you a gift, no matter how valuable

it might be, he did not mean for it to grow old along
with you. He expected you to use it when and as you
chose to honor someone else, and, indirectly, yourself.
He gave with that expectation, as much as to say,

"I have owned this for some time. You own it next,
and when you wish to make a gift, pass it on."

The teaching in the family, and in the *tiyośpaye*, was
definitely in the direction of giving. One patriarch,
when it came time to assemble gifts cooperatively to
honor their dead, admonished his group thus:

"My children, never skimp. Give adequately in a
manner worthy of yourselves, or not at all. Give abun-
dantly and with glorious abandon. Better not to honor
someone than dishonor him by doing it haltingly and
calculatingly. Pity the coward who gives half holding
back, timid for his own private security because he does
not put his faith in men but in mere chattel.

"My children, it is better to give and have nothing
left, if need be, than to appear stingy. Property always
flows back in due time to those who let it flow freely
forth. In the endless process of giving, that is bound
to be so."

Such was the inherited belief by which the Dakota
lived happy and satisfied all his days, and which he
handed down to his children. They had grown up with
it. Even the babies were imbued with it. "A man should
be able to give without his pulse quickening," was a
stock saying. The grateful recipients lauded the do-
nor's name before the people as having done well.

Before the Dakotas would appear small, they would

let everything go, calmly, recklessly, should the occasion demand it. When, for instance, a warrior died in battle, his respect-relatives (sisters and women cousins) withheld nothing that might enhance his glory and memorialize his name. When a baby was born or a relative died, and honoring ceremonies were in order, once again gifts flowed freely. It was customary at a death to "throw away" property—everything belonging to the deceased and anything else the relatives had that they deemed worth giving.

Outsiders will say, "In that case, people flocked to get presents?" Exactly, it was proper. The stricken family actually wanted friendly recipients for what they had to give away. And most callers did not come empty-handed either. They brought food to add to the feast, served silently or in tears to all who came to "help" wail. Dakotas did not want to mourn alone; they wanted relatives around them to help them.

There was little pride in ownership of goods, but much pride in "honorship" of relatives. If you wished to honor me publicly, you did not load me down personally with presents. You made someone else glad in my name—as though I were doing the giving—and that is where the honor lay for me. It brought three— the giver, the recipient, and me—rather than the usual two into closer relationship. Thus were kindness and good will generated even more broadly.

When mourners had thrown away goods and reduced themselves to temporary poverty, they still kept their dignity, even in an empty tipi, wearing the meanest of garb beside a cold hearth. For such a situation was no disgrace where riches were not an end. If anything, they were even surer of their prestige for it. Personal worth was not measured by what goods they had, but by what they could let go without flinching because of a dear one. "Only over the death of a human being are tears justified" was an adage. No man was so pitiful and wretched as one who did not conform to this practice and ideal.

This kind of apparent disregard, not to say disdain, for material things as against human considerations was the basis of the people's life and philosophy. I have dwelt perhaps disproportionately on it because it seemed important to show the radically different thought that motivated giving. But please do not thereby imagine there was nothing else in the people's economy or that they spent their days doing nothing but ridding themselves of property, as if it literally burned in their hands. That is not the impression I would leave, for that was not the case. There were actually intervals, sometimes long, when no occasion arose calling for gift-giving, and during such times the people enjoyed what they had and could acquire. The idea was, of course, that their code expected them "to act as men" whenever there was a human call to give—from their point of view as to what was a human call.

And now let us turn to the question of practical economics. In the first place, the Dakotas could not afford to be shiftless and wasteful in those days. The material basis of their life was all too slight, and the

danger of sudden famine always too imminent, for them
not to live frugally, utilizing everything possible in
the way of food. For centuries they had dehydrated
their food for long-keeping. They in common with
other tribes had known of a vast variety of wild foods,
both vegetable and animal, and the securing of them.
Besides foods, their knowledge of herbs and of their
medicinal values was also extensive.

They knew how to reduce bulk foods to their nutri-
tious essence for easy carrying—a knowledge important to a people ever on the move. Whenever there was
a great deal of meat, they jerked and dried all not required for immediate use by a process now practically
forgotten. They tenderized it while it was drying so
that when it was entirely dried the great thin sheets
were so pliable they could be folded almost like cloth
into flat packing cases for storing underground.

They made caches, great underground rooms which
were shaped like immense jars with narrow necks.
Down there, in a definite arrangement, the stores of
several cooperating families were piled around the
walls as high as might be. And, because it was necessary
that each woman know her own store and not confuse
it with others, her rawhide containers, which always
came in pairs, were boldly painted with her own over-
all design.

In this and similar ways the Dakotas practised
long-range planning. It goes without saying that now
and then they had a famine, when snow was too deep
for hunting, or when all the animals seemed to organ-

ize to keep out of their range. As a people, they did not dare let themselves drift into an easy, haphazard existence. They were wise in self-preservation, even though they were committed to constant hospitality, which they held to as long and as fully as possible.

The danger in explaining to outsiders the principle of giving-to-have is that it might appear as nothing more than a barter system. But really it was much finer than that. It had warmth and cordiality. Its spirit was gracious. It was of the very essence of Dakota communal life. If it were to stop suddenly for any reason, those who lived by it would be a lost people, a people without their bearings.

The giving system certainly was not for enriching oneself at the expense of others. A man who showed that tendency was suspect, as if he were not quite human. *Tak-taninśni* they said of him; meaning "What kind of thing (he may be) is not plain." The fact that gifts of unequal value were happily exchanged should give a clue that this was not just a bartering game. A horse for a beautiful pair of moccasins or a blanket was not unheard of. The recipient of the lesser gift might be so startled and delighted by the compliment thus unexpectedly paid him that he unhesitatingly gave a horse to indicate his pleasure.

All that I have been describing here in Part II concerns a life that went on before the white man came among the Dakotas. Yet I have personally observed enough in the vestiges of it still remaining to accept without question the accounts of it that have come down. I accept them, also, because I am sure of the personal integrity of my informants. Reflecting on the past people will naturally talk of the ideal. Good things are more easily remembered than the evil. That does not mean there wasn't a seamy side here as elsewhere. Of course there were those who cared naught for their reputation, who broke kinship laws, who habitually lived on the lowest plane. But they were not representative, so why must I waste wordage on them? If a visitor from Mars asked me about the American way of life, should I show him city slums or Sing Sing, or describe gangsterism to him, just because, unfortunately, there are such things? No, I should show him our churches, schools and colleges, and museums, and such theatre as I could be proud of. I should try to make him understand our democratic ideal and should hesitate to emphasize the particulars wherein we fall short of it as a nation.

It would not only be natural to show the best we have; it would be right.

Part III

The Reservation Picture

9: "THE OLD ORDER CHANGETH"

*As long as there are no stimuli that modify the social struc-
ture and mental life, the culture will be fairly stable. Isolated
tribes appear to us and to themselves as stable, because under
undisturbed conditions the processes of change of culture are
slow.—Franz Boas* [1]

IN THE OLD DAKOTA CULTURE THAT WE HAVE BEEN
observing the same things went on in the same way
from generation to generation, leaving nothing to be
desired. For the Dakota people, theirs was *the* way to
live; there was no other.

This does not imply that there was not a continuous
change in thought, but it was imperceptible; and, because it rooted in the culture, it offered no threat. New
ideas of art, especially in the matter of design, were
always appearing, "dreamed" by certain women whom

[1] From *Anthropology and Modern Life*. New York, W. W. Norton
& Co., 1932.

the tribe regarded as being supernaturally endowed.

Then, too, certain thinkers kept ahead of the masses in that they now and again caught an advanced idea and gradually introduced it. You recall how murderers were handled traditionally. Yet, once on a day, a man thought up the idea of making a relative of his kinsman's murderer, saw its worth, and was strong enough in his own *tiyospaye* to put it over the first time. Now and again, too, men discovered a new truth and harangued the people about it. Gradually there developed a body of aphorisms and folk sayings, such as "Let us think compassionately of woman, for she has to bear a pain that man can never know," or, "My kinsmen, this is true: hate kindles fire; kindness puts it out."

Take, too, the matter of the treatment of captives from other tribes. The rule, "Be kind to each other within the camp-circle, for it is sacred," implied that outsiders were something else. Accordingly, cruelty to captives was legitimate. And yet there were those who had come to feel sympathy for them, saying in effect: "He, too, has feelings, though he cannot speak Dakota. Be kind to him; he too is a man." But, as I said, these ideas were all growths from within. Not until there was outside pressure did Dakota culture undergo a real change.

It came, and without their asking for it—a totally different way of life, far-reaching in its influence, awful in its power, insistent in its demands. It came like a flood that nothing could stay. All in a day, it

seemed, it had roiled the peacefulness of the Dakotas'
lives, confused their minds, and given them but one
choice—to conform to it, or else! And this it could
force them to do because, by its very presence, it was
even then making their old way no longer feasible.

The arrival of the newcomers, the *Wasicu*, did not
appear as a threat at first. Now here, now there, singly
or in small groups, they began appearing in an infil-
tration that gained in size and momentum as it continued. Here were men of a different sort—incredible
curiosities, but harmless. They were a people with
strange, laughable ways. But those were their ways, so
let them be. Overlook it that their manners were bad;
they did make so many ingenious things, useful and
pleasant to have! Ingenious, clever, cunning, supernaturally efficient these newcomers were—hence their
name, *Wasicu*. The word carries no connotation of
"white." It means all the above things and is simply a
transfer of the name for one's helper in the spirit
world, one's mentor, peculiarly capable of impossible
feats through his superhuman cleverness and insight,
with a dash of trickery in it, legitimate for him, though
not for man.

On the whole, the general attitude was that it was
more good than bad, the *Wasicu's* coming, for as yet
it was not plain that some day he would be many and
the Dakotas would be few, or that his strange ways,
so incompatible to their own cherished ones, would prevail and they would have to bow to them.

And so for many years, even with white people about

in the land, the Dakota people were still able to live
pretty much in their own way. They still hunted the
rapidly diminishing buffalo. They still roamed, held
their old ceremonies, laid away their dead on scaffolds,
and fasted for visions. Eagerly they accepted *Wasicu*
articles, such as knives, guns, and woven goods, and
even introduced them into their rites for an innovation.
They started to wear flannel and calico for clothing,
though still cut after the old patterns of buckskin
dress, and succeeded in adapting the new imported
seed beads to supplement porcupine quill work, thus
making of beadwork a new art form. Little did they
realize that all these things were forerunners of sweep-
ing change.

In its approach, that change resembled somewhat a
midsummer thunder storm that gathers slowly. For a
time it appears to be only a black curtain hung clear
across the west, screening out the declining sun but
leaving the sky overhead an intense blue, clear and
calm. In reality it is a great storm, marshaling its
forces without haste as though making exact and
sinister plans so that when finally it gets into action,
it will be sure to make a thorough job of it—perhaps
even killing many.

But there my simile breaks down. For when a real
storm gathered thus slowly the people could see it and
get ready. With one eye on the cloud they could hustle
about to make their tipi more secure with extra guys,
weighing down the base with heavy logs and driving
the anchoring pegs still deeper into the ground. All

round the camp-circle they would do this, till even the most nonchalant would be moved to action, seeing everybody else getting ready so frantically.

The coming of the new order was not like that. It also took its time, but subtly. It gathered its forces out of sight, and it sneaked up on the people in a surprise attack that caught them entirely unprepared. Suddenly it struck. It struck hard—in the mass slaughter of the buffalo, in the Custer fight, in the killing of Sitting Bull, and, finally, in that ghastly incident at Wounded Knee, in 1890, when innocent men, women, and children were massacred. Those were the decisive blows, the death-dealing shafts hurled into Teton-Dakota life, the final reasons for change. The Wounded Knee massacre was occasioned by the Ghost Dance, of which I shall have more to say.

That a change was necessary not many can deny. A relatively small group of mankind could not rightly refuse to share their vast rich domain with others; they could not rightly prevent its exploitation for the good of the many. I do not think there is a Dakota who would doubt the rightness of that, if only he understood. But the way in which it happened was cruel.

It is all long past. Both those who did the injuries and those who bore them are gone. This is no useless tirade against former injustices. I speak of the things that brought on the change and hurried the people into reservation life only because they help in understanding subsequent developments.

As for the Ghost Dance and the religious ideas back

of it, it was a new thing, an importation from a tribe
farther west where it had grown out of that people's
bewilderment at the same kind of changes that were
touching the Dakotas.

It is not true that all the Dakotas accepted it, or
pinned their waning hopes on its promises. Actually
the Santee or eastern Dakotas, the Yankton or central
Dakotas, and many Teton or western Dakotas never
subscribed to it at all. They stood aloof, seeing it as
a pitiful effort leading nowhere, and were sorry for
those who had such faith in it. I once heard old Teton
and Yankton men talking about it together, ruefully,
in these words:

"It was hopeless and fantastic, from the start. Poor
and desperate even though we all were, it was foolish
to fall for it. They did not have to be slaughtered like
cattle and turned into a common grave for that!"

But those from four bands of the Teton who did
accept the cult, did so with tragic earnestness. Feverishly, at the eleventh hour, they instituted it as the
possible way out of their crisis. With Pine Ridge
agency already a going concern and with United
States soldiers waiting to be called out momentarily,
they dared against orders to continue their religious
dances, thinking thereby to turn the tide, somehow, by
supernatural means.

Some years ago, a man sixty years of age or more
gave me an account of the Ghost Dance as he saw it
through the eyes of a small boy of nine or ten. I translate freely:

It was over fifty years ago. A big new government school had been put up at Pine Ridge, and we were kept there, boys and girls *together*—an unheard-of thing. We wore *Wasicu* clothes, which neither fitted nor felt right on us. In fact, we looked terrible in them, but we had to wear them or be punished.

The rumor got about: "The dead are to return. The buffalo are to return. The Dakota people will get back their own way of life. The white people will soon go away, and that will mean happier times for us once more!"

That part about the dead returning was what appealed to me. To think I should see my dear mother, grandmother, brothers and sisters again! But, boylike, I soon forgot about it, until one night when I was rudely wakened in the dormitory. "Get up, put on your clothes and slip downstairs, we are running away," a boy was hissing into my ear.

Soon fifty of us, little boys about eight to ten, started out across country over hills and valleys, running all night. I know now that we ran almost thirty miles. There on the Porcupine Creek thousands of Dakota people were in camp, all hurrying about very purposefully. In a long sweat lodge with openings at both ends, people were being purified in great companies for the holy dance, men by themselves and women by themselves, of course.

A woman quickly spied us and came weeping toward us. "These also shall take part," she was saying of us. So a man called out, "You runaway boys, come here." They stripped our ugly clothes from us and sent us inside. When we were well purified, they sent us out at the other end and placed sacred shirts on us. They were of white muslin with a crow, a fish, stars, and other symbols painted on. I never learned what they meant. Everyone wore one magpie and one eagle

feather in his hair, but in our case there was nothing to tie
them to. The school had promptly ruined us by shaving off
our long hair till our scalps showed lighter than our faces!

The people, wearing the sacred shirts and feathers, now
formed a ring. We were in it. All joined hands. Everyone
was respectful and quiet, expecting something wonderful to
happen. It was not a glad time, though. All walked cautiously
and in awe, feeling their dead were close at hand.

The leaders beat time and sang as the people danced, going
round to the left in a sidewise step. They danced without rest,
on and on, and they got out of breath but still they kept
going as long as possible. Occasionally someone thoroughly
exhausted and dizzy fell unconscious into the center and lay
there "dead." Quickly those on each side of him closed the
gap and went right on. After a while, many lay about in that
condition. They were now "dead" and seeing their dear ones.
As each one came to, she, or he, slowly sat up and looked
about, bewildered, and then began wailing inconsolably.

One of the leaders, a medicineman, asked a young girl,
"My kinswoman, why do you weep?" Then she told him tear-
fully what she had just seen, and he in turn proclaimed it to
the people. Then all wailed with her. It was very dismal.

I remember two of the songs:

> "Mother, hand me my sharp knife,
> Mother, hand me my sharp knife,
> Here come the buffalo returning—
> Mother, hand me my sharp knife!"

> "Mother, do come back!
> Mother, do come back!
> My little brother is crying for you—
> My father says so!"

The visions varied at the start, but they ended the same way, like a chorus describing a great encampment of all the Dakotas who had ever died, where all were related and therefore understood each other, where the buffalo came eagerly to feed them, and there was no sorrow but only joy, where relatives thronged out with happy laughter to greet the newcomer. That was the best of all!

Waking to the drab and wretched present after such a glowing vision, it was little wonder that they wailed as if their poor hearts would break in two with disillusionment. But at least they had seen! The people went on and on and could not stop, day or night, hoping perhaps to get a vision of their own dead, or at least to hear of the visions of others. They preferred that to rest or food or sleep. And so I suppose the authorities did think they were crazy—but they weren't. They were only terribly unhappy.

So ends the account. It was indeed the pathetic final attempt to regain a paradise lost forever. The agency was jittery lest the people work themselves into a frenzy and fight again, and so they called out the military, and the Wounded Knee massacre was the result. After that, those who had adhered to the short-lived religion from the west did not dare to resume it. I cannot forbear repeating my informant's closing comment:

"For my part, I think it was not so bad as the Peyote cult today that keeps Indians half-doped all the time, making them all the easier prey for the crooked. They stopped the Ghost Dance; they ought to stop the peyote-eating, too!"

The news of the massacre quickly spread from

reservation to reservation, confirming what many wise Dakota leaders knew already: that the old way of life was gone forever and nothing could bring it back; it was as dead as the buffalo, the Ghost Dancers, and the murdered Sitting Bull—last symbol of Teton resistance. It was now clearly the better part of wisdom to try adjusting to the new way. The reservations had already been marked out a number of years before. On each there was an agency representing a remote power called a "Grandfather" under whose dictatorship they had somehow come to be. Why? They did not know. And they found it irksome, being under another's control when through countless generations they had always been free.

But they were a people used to accepting fate with fortitude and dignity. They still repeated their favorite adage, "Since it must be so, it is so," and they turned to the white man's way with remarkably little bitterness. Had they better understood what fundamentally must be done to make the change, they might have made better headway than they did. In retrospect we can see the mistakes, the stupidities, the indignities that made the going rough. At that they started out well enough, almost too well, with proverbial beginner's luck. The thoughtful and the objective were anxious for the future. The rank and file took each day as it came, preoccupied with the mere business of keeping alive under strange conditions.

Reservation life has never been a "still." It is a moving picture of continuous change. It has reacted readily to all sorts of stimuli from without, and these have come with increasing variety and frequency through the years, modifying the social structure and mental life of the people for better and for worse. The picture moves through time. Imagine it projected on a screen. In 1890 the scene is still very primitive. Even in 1900 it remains a predominantly Dakota picture, in spite of a scattering of log houses, schools, and churches. By 1910, drastic changes have come. Great transcontinental "flyers" speed shrieking through the once peaceful valley, jarring the ground under the tipis set up there for a Christian gathering. A yet higher peak of change is shown a few years later when World War I and cheap automobiles appear almost together. And now, today! War Birds darken the sky, and deafening sounds fill the air from the near-by bombing ranges that the Dakotas have loaned the War Department. Surely, this must be the all-time high of change! What will come from it all?

Cultural change moves through space as well as through time. It is, therefore, impossible to follow its spread, mile on mile, over the several Dakota reservations—nor even over one—for changes never happen uniformly. Each reservation has its centers of rapid change and its slower hinterlands. The most I can do in these chapters, then, is to give some random glimpses of life in these years of transition just as I tried to show the old Dakota life in Part II. All my material is factual, taken from my own observation or from what others have told me out of their knowledge.

Reservation life is a moving picture in still another sense—moving to those who watch it thoughtfully and sympathetically and who are naturally sensitive to the struggles of men against heavy odds. It moves me; I wistfully hope it will move you.

10: LIFE IN LOG CABIN AND ON ALLOTMENTS

WITH THE WHITE MAN IN THE LAND AND WITH the Dakotas now confined to reservations, the old way of life was rapidly untenable. The imaginary lines of demarcation, within which all those enrolled in each agency were ordered to remain, were regularly overpassed, unconsciously, and agency police were as regularly going out to bring the offenders back.

Such an offender was put in prison. Of course prison life was really only symbolic, for the prisoner lived with the police staff and worked certain hours at raking the superintendent's yard or at some such task. He chatted as he pleased in a leisurely and friendly way with passers-by. Imprisonment was without stigma to the Dakotas, who never imprisoned one another in the old life. One man did not arbitrarily keep another from his freedom. You did that only with horses or other animals, not fellow men. So there was actually no name for it but "to be tied up." "Yes," a woman camping near the agency during her husband's term might explain, "we are waiting here because their father [indicating the children] is tied up just now. When they untie him, we shall go home." There was no shame in the matter. But everything was very confusing. The people, not understanding, did some irrational things, irrational even from their own standpoint, for which they were sorry ever after. Some years ago, Standing Elk, an old man living at Rapid City, South Dakota, told me this story about his father's death:

During the time our people were kept camping at the agency and watched closely lest they get into the wild country and perhaps make war again, my aged father died. [He named a famous chief.] So his nephews requested leave to take his body out into the wilds for the burial rites, which they still adhered to. Certainly in his case it was the only choice. They had spent four days out there, mourning under the scaffold on which they had bound the body, when two men from the agency came to take them back. They had overstayed their pass.

The eldest nephew tried to explain why, but one of the messengers struck him an insulting blow and told him to stop talking and start back. A fight ensued, with the result that the two eldest nephews were put in prison. This time they were rudely thrown into close confinement. There they sang their war songs, feeling sorrowful and angry and deeply offended by the violence to their dignity and their given word. And they vowed that when they got out they would kill the first white man they met. And therein lay the tragedy.

Meantime the other relatives went to the new missionary, who was different from the usual type of white man. Would he help them? Of course! So this missionary immediately drove to the agency, explained the situation and effected the men's release. Riding home that evening, happy no doubt over having befriended the injured, he came down a lonely hill, crossed the stream, and started slowly up the next hill.

The two men who had been released that afternoon waited in ambush. Yes, it was a white man all right, driving in a little black buggy. They fired at him from behind, killing him instantly. Imagine how they felt when they learned that they had killed their own benefactor! They scarified themselves till the blood flowed free, and they mourned many days. They were never truly happy again.

Other clashes between the old way and the new happened regularly. The Dakotas used to bury their dead with necklaces of money and elk teeth for which there was demand commercially. Now burial scaffolds were being looted for what they might contain. And this violation forced the people into the dreaded new way of putting their dear ones under the ground. War dances lost their "kick" after intertribal warfare was forbidden. "Civilized men did not kill each other." Without any war deeds to extol, there was no longer any point to war dances. Ceremonies, too, were difficult to manage now, because of the cramped life forced on the people. When the sun dance, their greatest corporate ceremony, was stopped by the authorities because of the self-torture essential to it, the people gave it up. It would be pointless without sacrifice.

Finally, it was impossible to carry on the quest for visions in the traditional manner. It just did not seem as if there was one distant, solitary peak any more

where a man could fast unmolested. Almost always
some white man would come by to distract, often inno-
cently, the praying man. An old man once said to me
with a wry smile, "They sometimes mean well. But
whether with bad or good intent, they cannot help but
interfere with our way, because they cannot comprehend it. So we may as well adopt theirs. We cannot
live according to our way in their midst, that is
plain."

Then he went on to tell me about a man who tried
to fast in the early days of the reservation era. This
man was so distraught by the new conditions and so in
need of a great immediate revelation that he made himself suffer extraordinarily, in order to be sure of getting it. He passed a rope across his bare chest and
under his arms. Then he tied the ends fast to a tree
stump growing on the rim of a precipice, and let himself down. It was very painful to dangle there; the sun
burned him all day and the night air chilled him.
Moreover, he had even deprived himself of the permissible pipe. But it was the way he wanted it to be. And
now he was almost losing consciousness. Very soon he
would have his vision of the "Grandfathers." Then,
faintly and as if far away, he heard talking. Coming
to quickly, he looked up and saw over the edge of the
cliff a bearded white man whose blue eyes flashed with
righteous indignation. Shaking his head in abhorrence,
he struggled until he had pulled the praying man up.
The intruder's language was unintelligible, but his
manner and gestures were plain. "Who has done this

horrible thing to you? Tell me, and I will kill him with my gun!"

What was the use? Gone the imminent vision; wasted all that time and effort in courting it. His desperate attempts foiled, the would-be visionary rode back with the white man, disappointed, of course, but finding some comfort in the good intentions that led his rescuer to interfere.

It must be understood that all these customs and rites did not vanish overnight, but they were disappearing steadily under the pressure forcing the people into a sedentary life. For that was how they must live now, and it was a radical change indeed and far from easy. For unknown generations they had been on the move, and they liked it. They were deep in that groove, both physically and spiritually.

They made a brave, and, on the whole, a cheerful try at adapting themselves to the new ways, haphazard as their methods were. Being naturally stoical and realistic, they saw that since there were no more buffalo it was nonsensical to continue hunting; and that since free food was proffered them, they might as well sit down and eat it.

So they settled here and there, in *tiyospaye* clusters along the wooded streams—with nothing to do. Literally that, because they could not see what there was to do nor that any regular work was necessary. It was a devastation for a whole people. Why didn't they turn immediately to farming? Well, why should they do that, any more than anything else outside of hunting?

Of necessity they were overtrained specialists in that one thing, without time or chance for sidelines or avocations. Their habits as roaming hunters were almost unalterably fixed. It would take the most painstaking, patient, and understanding re-education to change their reflexes—a fact not always recognized by the sincere friends who wanted to save them; who naïvely imagined that a change of costume, and plough handles in the grasp, would turn the trick. But I no more blame these friends than I do the people themselves for not realizing what they were up against. Without perspective, how could they?

Eventually, with pathetic optimism, the Dakotas started putting up their first loghouses, patterned after those of the white man. They moved in and set up housekeeping, supposing it would be just that easy. They had not begun to understand all that goes with the new way of living they had adopted.

The houses were small, one-room affairs, low and dark—and dank, because of the dirt floors. Compared with the well constructed tipis with their manageable windflaps for ample ventilating, the cabins were hot and stuffy. Germs lurked everywhere, causing general sickness, and the death rate increased. Even if the hygiene necessary for controlling the spread of sickness had been explained to them, a conflict would have arisen between its demands and the ancient concern for kinship. "What? Am I to shun my dear ones just because they are ill, in order to save my own self?" It was unthinkable. And so, for many years it seemed as if this were the finish. But the Dakotas were not panicky. At the same time that they loved life passionately, ending many ancient prayers with, "Wise Grandfather, may I live long!" a defiance of death to the point of flippancy was also in their code. "Am I to die? Good! So much the sooner I can see my grandmother again!" was a familiar deathbed retort.

At length there came the time when individual allotments of land were made. Families were encouraged to live out on them and start to be farmers forthwith. Equipment for this, as well as some essential furniture, was given the most docile ones by way of inducement. But again, it wasn't easy to make the spiritual and social adjustment. The people were too used to living in large family groups, cooperatively and happily. Now, here they were in little father-mother-child units (with an occasional grandparent, to be sure), often miles from their other relatives, trying to farm an arid land—the very same land from which, later on, white farmers of Old World tradition and training could not exact even a subsistence living. Enduring frightful loneliness and working at unfamiliar tasks just to put himself ahead financially were outside the average Dakota's ken. For him there were other values. The people naturally loved to foregather; and now the merest excuse for doing so became doubly precious. For any sort of gathering it was the easiest thing to abandon the small garden, leave the stock to fend for themselves, and go away for one to four weeks. On returning, they might find the place a wreck. That was too bad; but to

miss getting together with other Dakotas was far
worse.

After a time, however, they were making better,
larger houses—neater, too, with the logs planed so as
to fit closer and requiring less of the mud chinking that
was always coming loose in the first cabins. The doors
and windows fitted better, there were floors, and the
roofs were of boards. The people began to make ingenious adaptations of some elements in their old life
to the new. For instance, at one period they trans-
ferred the art decorations of the tipi to the loghouse.
Out of G.I. muslin they made very large wall-cover-
ings, a carry-over from the dew-curtain of a tipi and
called by the same term, *ozan*. On these they painted
beautiful designs and made lively black-and-white
drawings of historical scenes of hunting or battles or
peace-making between tribes, and courtship scenes,
games, and suchlike activities of the past. People went
visiting just to see one another's pictographs and to
hear the stories they preserved. I barely remember one
such wall-covering which had been given to be sold,
the proceeds to be used for missionary work. My father
brought it home, and my mother had it hung so that
the teachers at the school might see it. It was large
enough to cover most of two sides of our fourteen-by-
fifteen-foot dining room in the rectory. This interesting mode of decoration passed out quite suddenly when
it became the fashion, perhaps about 1908, to build
frame houses.

My impression is that the women took especial pride

in caring for their new homes and new furniture. Once my mother took me along to call on Nancy Gall, daughter of the famous chief, and we found her vigorously scrubbing her pine floor to a brilliant yellow and cleaning house generally. "I promised the *tiwahe-awanyaka* [guardian-of-the-family] to do this every Floorwashing Day [Saturday], and I have never missed yet!" she explained, rising from her knees to greet my mother.

A salute right here to the government field-matrons, those guardians-of-the-family! Attached to the agency staffs, they did a great deal of good in helping the women to a fine start and inspiring them to learn. It was a pity they were withdrawn, for, in a way, they were the most constructive influence exerted by government at that period. They were no Home Ec. Ph.D.'s, that's true. They were only sensible, motherly women, usually elderly, with *hearts that were right*. And that, I think, is nearly enough in practical work with so-called backward peoples. Feeling their warmth and sympathy, the people responded well in numerous cases and spoke of them later on with respectful gratitude. Among other things, those women taught the Dakota housewives to make "lung bread," as yeast-raised bread was named because of the air holes. Formerly only baking-powder dough was known, but now there was a definite preference for the new kind. The field-matrons taught many. Others made long journeys to our mission to be taught there.

I can imagine the delight of the husbands when their

wives wished to make the trip. With what sudden
alacrity they must have stepped around, getting the
team hitched to the wagon! To their monotonous
new life, it was a welcome break to get together with
other men also camping around the mission for one
reason or another. "We are here while *winunhca* learns
how to make lung bread." So they would account for
themselves, temporarily happy again, as they sat in
circles upon the ground to smoke the endless pipe and
talk about past glories.

They needed those breaks, poor things! It was they
who suffered the most from the enforced change,
whether they realized it or not. It was their life primarily that was wrecked; it was their exclusive occupation that was abruptly ended. The women could go
right on bearing children and rearing them. They
could cook, feed their families, set up and strike camp
unaided, pack and unpack when on a trip. Even em-
broidery, exclusively a woman's art, was not cut off
suddenly. It tapered away as the buffalo and deer skins
on which the work was done became more and more
scarce. By slow degrees, meanwhile, they could learn
other work and were able to make the shift more easily.

The man was the tragic figure. Frustrated, with his
age-old occupation suddenly gone, he was left in a
daze, unable to overcome the strange and passively
powerful inertia that stayed him from doing anything
else. And so he sat by the hour, indifferent and inactive, watching—perhaps envying—his wife, as she
went right on working at the same essential rôle of

woman that had been hers since time immemorial. In
such a mental state, what did he care that unsympa-
thetic onlookers called him "lazy Indian" and accused
him of driving his wife, like a slave, while "he took his
ease"! As though he enjoyed it! If, as he sat there,
someone had called, "Hey! There's a herd of buffalo
beyond that hill! Come quick!" he would have sprung
into life instantly again. But, alas, no such thing would
ever happen now. All he could do, or thought he could
do, on his "farm" was to water the horses mechani-
cally, bring in fuel and water, cut a little hay, tend a
little garden. He did it listlessly, almost glad when the
garden died on his hands for lack of rain. His heart
was not in what he was doing anyway—until something
human came up: a gathering of the people, where he
could be with many relatives again; or a death, when
he must go to help with the mourning; or a cow to be
butchered, reminiscent of the hunt; or time to go to
the agency for the biweekly issue of rations. That he
must not miss. For him and his family, that was what
still gave meaning to life.

Kinship continued strong, in spite of the dispersion,
and the people had all the time in the world now for
honoring each other, and for the giving of courtesy
food and goods with still the same fervor. This was, in
a way, the golden age for giving, for there was more
to do with—yards of G.I. goods, numerous items of
rationed foods (as if they didn't all have the same
amounts to begin with!), and beautiful silver dollars,
ideal gifts to seal a handshake—sometimes with a mur-

mured, "My relative, with this I shake your hand," but, just as often, transferring it from palm to palm without a word.

Going after rations involved several days, with pleasant camps en route, depending on how far away a family lived from the agency. Traveling in company, as in olden days, packing a tipi and other essential equipment and starting out leisurely, and at the last arriving to form one great camp-circle once more for three or four precious days—that was living! The intervening times were waiting times. Drawing rations was almost incidental.

Rations are now an old story to the Dakotas. Each family received food in quantities according to its size and carried a ration card to be presented at the gate. For people unaccustomed to such procedure, they did this with surprising conformity. Recently I felt troubled about the old people and their rations points, because I heard so much grumbling about them here in New York. If these city people who read can fuss so much, our poor old Dakotas must be having a terrible time, I thought. But when I wrote out to ask, my friend reassured me. "You'd be surprised," she said. "They do better than many of us who can read, once the English instructions are interpreted to them." Then she added this amusing bit. Some frivolous young women were trying to work an old man who, they knew, had some cash. "Uncle, we are so meat-hungry. Why don't you buy us a steak?" they teased him.

They needn't have. For he was still faithfully observing kinship laws. When someone called him "Uncle," that immediately put him in a protective and responsible attitude, and made him want to comply with whatever the request might be, at any personal cost. He said at once, "Certainly, my Nieces, if you are meat-hungry, by all means order as much as you'd like, and I will pay for it." And then he hastened to add dryly, "But *your* meat points, not mine!"

So, after all, a native shrewdness in meeting new conditions has not died in all these years of enforced dormancy. I think that's encouraging.

11: CHRISTIANS OF THE FIRST GENERATION

IN THE FULLNESS OF TIME, JUST WHEN THE TETON-Dakotas needed a friend, the church came to them, as, approximately thirty years earlier, under remarkably similar circumstances it had come to the Santees, their fellow Dakotas in Minnesota.

I have tried to show how white civilization had hit Teton-Dakota life with cruel impact and thrown it into wild confusion. But now all was still once more—with the stillness of defeat. It was as though, after being sucked without warning into a remorseless whirlpool and helplessly lashed and bruised by the wreckage pounding around them, the people had at last been thrown far off to one side and were sitting there, naked and forspent, dully watching their broken life being borne along, and lacking both the strength and the will to retrieve any of it. And what good was it now anyway, in pieces? The sun dance—without its sacrificial core; festive war dances—without fresh war deeds to celebrate; the Hunka rite of blessing little children— without the tender Ring of Relatives to give it meaning —who would want such empty leavings? No, it was better just to get along somehow without.

But it left them lonely, with an ache in the heart and an emptiness of soul. And then the church came and filled that emptiness to overflowing. When next you hear anyone question the depth of Dakota Christianity, implying it is only a veneer, a convenient exterior, don't you believe it! It is their very life. I know, because it was already going strong when I was old enough to remember, and I grew up watching its working all about me.

It may be different or similar with the various other tribes; that is for those who know other situations to tell. I have to get very personal here and tell you what I myself know. The mission that I know best happens to be that of the Episcopal church; but the situation is doubtless much the same with the work of the Congregational and the Presbyterian churches as well as the Roman Catholic, for those were the Christian bodies that came to the Dakotas and faithfully stayed by them throughout the years. I do not concentrate on the work of my own church for any other reason than that by doing so I can give you first-hand glimpses of what happened there. I am mindful of and grateful for all the good that has been accomplished by all Christian missions everywhere.

The masses of people accepted the church eagerly. But certain ones, like Chief Gall who lived a mile from the mission, took a long time to study out the gospel message with care and to appraise it critically. I am told that at the beginning Gall always came to church painted up as for a war council, looking austere and a little frightening. The young clergyman knew he was on trial, he and his message. Gall would sit by the door with his weapons—he never came without them—and would watch every move the minister made in the chancel and take in every word he uttered, with a grimly searching look that was disconcerting. At any minute if the missionary had said something that seemed off key, Gall might just as well have finished him off then and there in the interest of his people. (Who is this mere boy, all dressed up in white and talking to deceive us? I will get rid of him!) But in the end, he made a great feast with the clergyman as his honor guest. When all had eaten and smoked the pipe together, he spoke to him in a public oration, calling him *misun*, "my younger brother"—a social kinship term, certainly, since Gall was a Teton of the Tetons, while the clergyman was a prince of the Yanktons, another dialect division:

Misun, for many moons I have sat at your *wihuta* [the seat by the doorway; a term denoting the humblest space in a tipi] and listened with critical attention to all you say. And now I have some conclusions. What you tell us this man Jesus [pronounced Jeh-zoos] says we must do unto others, I already know. Be kind to your neighbor, feed him, be better to him than to yourself, he says. All are brothers, he says. But that's an old story to me. Of course! Aren't we all Dakotas? Members one of another, he says. *Misun,* do you know any cluster of Dakota people who are not linked together in kinship? If anyone wants you to escort him part way, take him to his very tipi door. If he asks for your shirt, by all means give him your blanket also, he says. Well, all that I have always done, and I know it is good. But now he also says, Love your enemies, for they are your brothers. And he says, if someone strikes one cheek, let him strike the other, too. That I have never done. That I have to learn, hard as it sounds.

What is entirely new to me is that the Wakan is actually the Father of all men and so he loves even me and wants me to be safe. This man you talk about has made Wakantanka very plain to me, whom I only groped for once—in fear. Whereas I once looked about me on a mere level with my eyes and saw only my fellow man to do him good, now I know how to look up and see God, my Father, too. It is *waśté* [well].

And so Gall was baptized and confirmed; and all his days he received special instruction from time to time, calling the missionary in to have things clarified ever and again. He was not just grabbing at externals. He was a student of Christ's teachings. A man of tremendous influence, he inspired many. When he died he was buried in consecrated ground, and a stone in the mission cemetery marks his grave to this day.

Other striking stories of conversion, some as sudden

as St. Paul's, and some preceded by slow careful weighing, are told. This is only one. The gospel had come, fresh and new and enlightening, and because its social message was already partially familiar, there was a sound foundation for the structure of Dakota Christianity. The Good News banished fear of the elements, it extended man's duty to his neighbor beyond tribal limits, and it showed him God in the face of Jesus Christ. Imagine how wonderful to hear it all for the first time!

And their hearing of the word of God was not dependent upon the varying forms in which their religious leaders might be able to cast it as they spoke; now they could hear it over and over again in the same precise words each time it was *read*, for behold, there it was ready for them in the Dakota language. Parts of the New Testament had been translated by 1840 and it was completed in 1865. The whole Bible was ready by 1879.

I have to stop and tell something of what lay behind that work of translation. It was a monumental undertaking; and all must bow gratefully to those Congregational and Presbyterian missionaries who first reduced Dakota speech to writing and then put years of work into the preparation of the texts. It is a story full of romance. First of all, there were the Pond brothers, self-appointed and self-sent, who in 1834 came from New England to the Santee-Dakotas near the present Twin Cities and almost at once began transcribing the language phonetically. They did a

great deal to lay the groundwork for Dr. Stephen
Return Riggs, Dr. Thomas S. Williamson, and their
colleagues of the following years.

And now picture this scene drawn from contempo-
rary records. It is a log house, ample and many
roomed, for it is the home of the French and Dakota
fur trader, Renville, a man of keen intellect, though
without any schooling to speak of and without any
fluency in English. In a bare room with flickering
candlelight he sits hour on hour of an evening after a
hard day of manual work. Dr. Riggs and his helpers
are across the table from him. They are working on the
translations. It is a blessing incalculable for all Dakota missions that Drs. Williamson and Riggs are
scholars. One of them reads a verse—in Hebrew, if it
is from the Old Testament, or in Greek, if from the
New. He ponders its essence, stripped of idiom, and
then he gives it in French. Renville, receiving it thus
in his father's civilized language, now thinks it through
very carefully and at length turns it out again, this
time in his mother's primitive tongue. Slowly and pa-
tiently he repeats it as often as needed while Dr. Riggs
and the others write it down in the Dakota phonetics
already devised by the Pond brothers. To me that is a
thrilling picture with far-reaching implications for the
culture of a whole people.

And it was that Bible so laboriously made, via the
French rather than the English route, that all the
Dakota peoples, first Santees, then Yanktons, and
eventually Tetons, received with unbounded eagerness.

Trained from of old to retain whole legends and year-counts verbatim, they were able to memorize long passages—because on each reading they heard it in exactly the same words. Of course it was the Santee dialect, but any Dakota can understand all dialects while keeping strictly to his own. A Yankton and a Teton couple can live together all their lives and converse freely, yet never compromise their respective dialects. It is, in the main, a matter of consonant shifts, and a Dakota can make those shifts as he reads. Where a wholly new word comes up, its meaning is soon learned and the equivalent substituted. Occasionally the same word may have different meanings but they too are quickly explained.

I want now to cut back to my mention of Christianity's banishing fear of the elements. In the early days a poor woman had a Heyoka dream, and wept in terror each time there was a cloud in the sky. Heyoka ceremonies, wherein the victim acted in a foolish manner to appease the thunders or be killed, had not then been performed for some years. But she was still a pagan and still believed she would be struck by lightning for not demonstrating her dream publicly. Yet there was no place to do it, for the people were living scattered about; and there was no audience, for her neighbors were now preponderantly Christian.

She was told to go to the minister. Maybe he could help her. She went to him, all jittery and sobbing with fright, for a great storm was gathering even then. He talked to her gently, using kinship terms, telling her

not to fear and that Christians did not fear the
thunders since they had no power of themselves.

"Sit here near me," he said, "and we will watch the
storm until it passes. It will not harm you for not acting out your dream—now or ever!" She sat there,
preferring the floor from habit, but crouched close to
his chair, so that any shaft aimed at her must hit him
too, it would seem. Whenever there was a flash she
shuddered pitifully and could not look up. But when
the storm had passed in due time, the woman was cured
of her fears. Eventually she became a Christian, a real
one, who all her days lived as consecrated a life of
gratitude as was ever lived.

Through trouble and tears, pleasure and laughter,
the church has stood by the people, and it must be said
that in their devotion they have stood by it, too. It has
meaning for them; it functions even in their social life.
Never is there a meal but grace is said first in all reverence. Never a feast or an hour of games or even a
political meeting but a church service precedes it.
That is habit; it has been from the beginning. Only
the other day, I heard of a woman who came late to
work at a mission in western South Dakota and explained the reason.

"I was so sleepy. Lawrence was going off to war on
the early train. So we got up at three in the morning
and ate breakfast. Then his father had prayers, and
then we started for town."

I know that father. He is a very ordinary layman,
and he never made any pretensions as a religious leader

among his people. Yet, quite as a matter of course, he reads prayers before he sends his boy off to war. What a way to do! If all fathers did that, would it not be something for the boys to think back on as they face the enemy? Nor is that an isolated case. It is the kind of thing they do without stopping to debate the matter.

Among Episcopalians the church year is very definitely ordered, with its sequence of feasts and observances starting from Advent. The people were already familiar, before my day, with the Dakota translations for the seasonal names, used them freely, and understood what they represented. They followed through with the proper collects, epistle, and gospel selections and read their teaching very carefully, for many had by this time learned to read. They sang appropriate hymns of the church seasons, some of which their own religious leaders had composed. Notably there is one hymn whose author was the first Dakota priest back in the early seventies. Its theme runs, "Kinship is a good thing; God devised it; let us all remember to live according to it." It identifies Christian brotherhood with the old Dakota kinship system and its laws of interpersonal responsibility and loving kindness, which of course is right. To me, that is the most typical of all Dakota-made Christian hymns.

Missionary work was not neglected either. The Santees in Minnesota, first to become Christians, sent missionaries westward to the Yanktons. The Yanktons in turn sent missionaries westward to the Tetons. And now the Tetons who had heard the gospel were sending lay missionaries to other Tetons who as yet had not heard it. Whenever there was an election of officers, there were several chosen "to take good news." These Christians, at their own expense, enthusiastically made regular journeys to the outlands, where they held meetings and passed on to the people what they knew. The people, in true Dakota style, feasted them royally first and then heard their message.

Even before they could read and write, the people elected the officers of their general church organizations and woman's auxiliary according to parliamentary procedure, Dakota brand. This was something that did not come out of their former life. It was a new thing, yet they took to it readily. They nominated, one at a time, seconded the nomination, then voted, for and then against. If those for were more than those against, the nominee won. Otherwise he was out, and the next name was put up. It took a long time, but there was lots of time.

In all earnestness, and with a genuine desire to help others, the people worked to raise money by making things to sell and in other ways. It is significant, however, that, until very lately, food sales were not resorted to. They clashed too badly with Dakota hospitality. The fund grew throughout the year. Then there came the day of apportioning it, before going to annual convocation to report. They had a meeting in which their clergyman read off to them the various projects they regularly helped and the special emergency calls for that particular year.

And so, "for work across the water" and "work at home" they sent money to national headquarters in New York, and to the state headquarters, for "The Bishop's Discretion," "The Fire Society" (which was insurance), "The Native Clergy Fund," and I do not recall what all. Special gifts were voted for the "Starving Armenians," the "Earthquake in Japan," the "Famine in China," as the needs arose. It was nothing new, helping others; it was something very new and very wonderful to extend that help far round the world. The most unlettered, retiring Dakota women helped as well as the more advanced. They still do.

I could talk on for pages more about these things. This is enough, I think, to show how easily the church took hold and why; why the people love it today and make it the whole of their life. If the missionaries and their kind of white people were all the Dakotas were ever to know, it would have been fine. Godlessness, irreverence, swearing, or boastful disbelief—such confusing things they did not come in contact with for years and years and hardly knew they existed. It was a decided shock when first some white travelers broke into the church to seek shelter from a terrible storm. That part was all right, but the trouble was that they allowed their children to play over the chancel furniture, break down the fragile shelf that answered for a credence table, and create havoc generally.

Those Dakotas are very devout. They do not talk foolishly, or even just sociably, within the church proper. Their veneration of the sacred mysteries and the outward symbols of them is a truly beautiful thing, satisfying in its absoluteness. Nor is that a new trait. From far in the past they were used to stepping lightly where solemn rites went on, to sense at once what was holy ground, and quickly "take off their shoes."

Here then is one picture of the transfer from the old religion to the new. You will see that it was no problem, that instinctively the people themselves dropped whatever was in conflict with it and retained those fine elements from the past that were fundamentally right as a firm foundation for the Christian life. If you could watch a Christian Dakota die, as I have, calm and full of faith and trust, you could never say, without being grossly unfair to Dakota Christianity, that it is only a veneer.

12: THE NEW EDUCATION

IF THERE ARE DAKOTAS LIVING TODAY, UNDER SIXTY-five and with normal intelligence, who have not at some time in their earlier years learned to write at least their names, and could not do it again if necessary, they must be in a very small minority. On the other hand, if there are any under twenty-five who read Dakota text with any sort of fluency, they too must be in the minority.

Education came to the Dakotas in two ways: through the formal school for the young, and through informal camp teaching for the adult.

Let's talk about the latter first. After the first white men arrived it suddenly dawned upon the people, to their amazement, that little marks on a sheet of paper could have meaning and could be read, and that the reading would run consecutively on, as if one were actually talking. That was thrilling enough. But as these years of change passed, it became possible not only to read out of the Holy Book, the hymnal, the *Book of Common Prayer*, and the other few translations now available, but it was also possible for *anybody* to write! A book called *The King's Highway* and another which I faintly recall hearing read, and judge now it may have been adapted from *Pilgrim's Progress*, were some of the other books being put out by the Riggses at their fine Congregational school at Santee, Nebraska, where the work of making Dakota a literary language went on apace. These were distributed among Dakota missions of all denominations for them to use. To my father's work they were of endless value.

Learning to write was laborious but fascinating. The most promising and eager men and women came to the mission centers—this was true everywhere—and were systematically taught; and then they turned around and taught others, informally, in camp. Men meeting anywhere might strike up such a conversation as this:

"Uncle, can you write?"

"Oh, yes, I now write very well!"

"Will you teach me how?"

"Of course, my Nephew."

If they had been riding, they would just as likely stop anywhere on the prairie and drop the bridle reins to let the horses graze, while they flopped down on the ground and began writing, their hats pushed back and their noses almost on the paper. Assiduously, then, they went to work, really "game" to learn. "He can write. He can't." It got to be a mark of differentiation, though without any reproach. Some simply hadn't tried, that was all. It was a new thing, and some people do not rush into new things.

In time reading and writing became quite general among the people. These new capacities affected many phases of their life, among them, of all things, courtship. A young man formerly used to halt a young girl going along, detain her, and talk with or rather to her, trying to persuade her that she was *the one*. But she would only laugh. She was taught never to commit herself, never to take a man's words seriously. If he really wanted her, he would do the manly thing— give gifts as a token of his wish, before all the people, and run the risk of her turning him down. Sometimes, because of bashfulness, such one-sided conversations did not get very far. Now, at last, a man could be as eloquent as he liked—on paper.

But courtship always was and is yet, except possibly for the very modern, a most controlled, dignified, and subtle affair. How to pour out one's heart and still be sure to remain dignified and to keep one's secret became a problem. It was not the custom for a suitor to deliver his own love letter. He would entrust it to a friend, who, in turn might have to relay it to others. All too likely, then, some young practical jokers would enjoy its contents along the way. Yet somehow those letters reached their destination, not infrequently with agreeable results in lasting marriages.

In essence the story of Dakota literacy is that of a new education that spread through informal camp teaching. The ability to read God's word for themselves in their own familiar tongue was of inestimable benefit. The power to communicate with one another by letter, both locally and across long distances with relatives on other reserves, was a tremendous advantage, too. But having gone that far, the new accomplishment seemed to stall. Further uses for it did not generally appear. As a medium of thought exchange with the non-Dakota world, it was ineffectual; and, after all, that was the urgency.

When the first enthusiasm passed, adult interest in learning to write slowly waned in inverse proportion to the growing ability of their young to do so. "My little boy can write now; I needn't exert myself longer," a parent might say. It had never been any too simple. There was no tradition for it, and most of the people had tried it too late in life. They began to throw their pencils aside and depend on the school children.

But the children were in most cases better versed in writing English and found that easier than trying to write Dakota. Some of the letters resulting from the youngsters' attempts to put their elders' ideas on paper have been marvels of interpretation. Some dignified old grandfather, proud and confident, would dictate formal words to a distant relative whom he wished especially to honor. There he would sit with eyes shut, the better to compose fine sentences, while his overrated grandchild struggled to translate and transcribe the involved speeches into English. "And now, dear relative, it is enough; I will now cease to address you for this time," might come out as, "Well, so long, friend, I have to ring off now."

No child would mean to be flippant with his grandfather's letter. He would be doing his level best, imitating something he had heard. Of course the old man would assume it was perfect. Fortunately at the other end another school child was sure to read the recipient's letter to him, and he couldn't help turning it into good Dakota idiom, for that was all that was possible to do. It wasn't funny to him either. And so the old timers imagined they had addressed each other with their habitual dignity, and never guessed the metamorphoses their serious sentiments had undergone en route. Such were some of the milder casualties in the struggle with acculturation.

And now let's talk about formal school education. On my table lie many letters and English exercises, on aging paper but written in readable and often perfect script. Variously dated from 1892 to 1910, they are the work of Dakota children. They reflect the best kind of teaching, with great emphasis on fundamentals, and the best kind of response on the part of the children. And they are little short of miraculous when we realize that hardly ten years prior to 1892, the parents of those particular children were only then trickling in from among the "hostiles" to the newly defined reservation limits, there reluctantly to settle down, for good and all, in a new and different way.

Those papers indicate happy, eager children, alert to whatever subject was introduced to them. The exercises reflect thorough teaching in geography, grammar, arithmetic. The compositions speak of good times: gathering spring crocuses, visiting parents in camp, the weekly "playnight" when boys and girls played together. "The lovely Easter will soon be here," says one, "and we are getting new Easter dresses." "Our teachers are so kind," says another.

They speak, too, of bread- and cake-making, of hemstitching, mending, and cleaning—all quite naturally. They write up the weekly Bible lesson, putting into English what the clergyman said in Dakota at church. Because they must do this, they pay strict attention. One writes, "If I say I will give you a nice book, is that a *promise?* Like that, God *promises* us life."

They have to give orally each day a detailed account of their morning's activities, as a means of acquiring ease in speaking English, so they write out samples of these: "Before prayers I opened my bed; after breakfast I made my bed. Then I helped to clear off the children's tables, pared potatoes, and got ready for school." They talk of going to church as an exciting experience, and of the new extension in the chancel to accommodate a choir, and of memorizing the weekly collect and learning to chant the canticles. (Chanting, I may add, comes easily to all Dakotas, for it is so like their own songs in which several words are sung on a sustained note.)

I just have to add this last, because it came as a surprise to me. I have known in later life some of those who wrote the first letters, and among them was one who seemed apparently little influenced by his short stay in school. But now I read some letters—of condolence, mind you—which they wrote to the relatives of their beloved principal, whose father had died back East at a time when she could not leave her work to go home. Sweet, kind, comforting letters they are. One girl with more candor than judgment does say, "Of course he was very old. It was time for him to die. We all have to die." But the other letters are all more in keeping, written with gentle tact. And the crowning sentiment is this: "My father is dead; so I *know* how it is." Think of that, written by one who in later life appeared not to have had any schooling at all. I should not have guessed that he once expressed so beautifully in English sentiments so characteristically Dakota.

"And often for each other, flows
The sympathizing tear."

Dakota children, hardly out of barbarism, comforting and sympathizing with friends of another race, whom they never hoped to meet! To me that is quite beautiful.

It would seem that in that splendid school hardly
a thing was omitted that might stimulate the children's
interest, broaden their knowledge, and give them
Christian nurture. The main point is that they were
taking it in so early; indeed, that they had the
capacity to take it in, and in English. A marvelous
start, rosy with promise! The Dakota child was a
sponge for new ideas then. Nor is this school picture an
isolated one. I suspect it might have been duplicated
in all the mission schools of all the churches engaged
in work among this tribe—and among others, too. I
cannot present the government school picture, either
on or off the reservation, in such detail, because I never
entered one, even to visit, until after my college days.
But of mission schools I know whereof I speak.

In considering formal school, we must remember
that the average Dakota child entered school like one
deaf. He had first to hear the English sounds, then
make sense out of them, and finally learn to speak. The
language handicap was the initial hurdle. There were
others. The fact that he had to learn industrial work
too and could attend classes only half a day was among
them. Far from blaming the Dakota child for being
behind in his grades, one should give him credit for
making such headway as he did make under the circumstances.

But now some real clashes happened between old and
new ideas. This was true in all schools, mission or
government. If a child called "Brother" someone entered on the roster as of an entirely different family,

was he lying? It seemed so, because the intricacies of his kinship system had not yet been investigated. Again, if brothers and sisters were told to dance or perform together and they held back, they were considered stubborn and disinterested in school. But it was only that a brother and sister were in respect-relationship, and part of the formal behavior required that they politely keep apart.

Language peculiarities also played havoc with a Dakota child in school. "You won't do that again, will you?" asked a teacher, correcting a child. "Yes," said the child each time the question was repeated. "Well, of all perversity!" thought the teacher, and perhaps punished the child. But the trouble was that in Dakota you say "yes" to a question like that, when in English you say "no." English says, "No (I will not)." Dakota says, "Yes (you are right that I will not)." Other language snags, just as simple if understood, made complications.

But I think the greatest interference with education was and has always been kinship and its duties. That splendid thing in the old life that held the tribe together beautifully in mutual deference and affection, remained to complicate matters for the young as they tried to get on in school. From the start, it challenged them again and again—and generally won out. A boy runs away, not necessarily because he dislikes school, but because someone has said that his mother is sick, and so he cannot rest until he knows for sure. Or a student in advanced training at one of our larger government schools might receive just before his final examinations a letter reporting that his father is dying. The successful passing of those examinations would place the student in a good position. But he insists that he must go. In vain the authorities remonstrate with him kindly.

"If you finish first, then you can do more for your people later. Don't you know you are throwing away your big chance?"

He knows that; none better than he. But he is both adamant and inarticulate. Some things lie too deep and too near the feelings to be analyzed and explained. "They wouldn't be understood anyway." That old ideal, that relatives and their needs and happiness come first, now enters in. The student knows he will be thought a fool. But he can stand that much better than he can resist the pull to go home.

"If my father is sick, I must go to him. Even if I make only his last hour happy, that is enough for me. What price my graduating and getting on top, if, to do it, I must ignore my filial duty?"

The thought preys on his mind night and day and he cannot even study for the finals. He goes home instead.

"What's the matter with him? I thought he was so fine," they say after he has left. "Well, that's an Indian for you! They're all alike. They lack ambition and pride in achievement." If they only knew the inner conflict, those who say that!

All his life, such a boy might have to dig with his

hands just because he did not qualify at that particular time. So be it! If ever he thought about it, he would reason, not, "I should have stayed," but, "It happened just then; so of course I could not stay." But, likely, out of loyalty he would never say any of it in words. He would make himself think it was right.

The education picture has changed slowly. The kinship system—so hard to deal with because it is so linked with dear ones—has been a retarding factor, but even so, many Dakotas have been to college and a good number are now holders of degrees.

What I have pictured here primarily concerns those who, as part of reservation life, are subject to kinship's sway. They are the ones who have found it hardest. It does not refer particularly to the many whose families have regularly lived elsewhere—among other tribes, or as employees of non-reservation schools, or have been urbanized for many years and no longer feel themselves an integral part of reservation social life. They come back to visit and are always welcomed as relatives. But they are not fundamentally controlled by the kinship way of life.

13: ECONOMICS: GETTING TO HAVE

THE AIM OF THE OLD DAKOTA ECONOMIC SYSTEM AND that of the white man's are one and the same, incongruous as that sounds when we compare the two systems for achieving it. Security, that was the aim:

food, clothing, shelter, and an old age free from want. All peoples need that; it is what they struggle for in their respective ways.

But the two systems in question are irreconcilable. They go counter to each other. One says in effect: "Get, get, get now; all you can, as you can, for yourself, and so insure security for yourself. If all will do this, then everyone will be safe." And it depends on things, primarily.

The other said: "Give, give, give to others. Let gifts flow freely out and they will flow freely back to you again. In the universal and endless stream of giving this is bound to be so." And that system depended on human beings—friends, relatives.

Both were and are consistent and workable within their own setting. But, today, the second system seems to be outmoded. In a world committed wholly to the other, it is out of place. It has to go. It goes reluctantly; indeed, it lingers and lingers still. It lingers because it is bound up with the kinship system, and that is still here. Kinship, as I have tried to show, was the whole of life in the past. It was what united the people. It insured friendship, kindness, courtesy, mutual helpfulness, and all the nice warm things that cheer the heart.

In other words, it is kinship, that splendid bond of the past, that now interferes whenever a Dakota tries to break away from the old economic order to the new. Kinship, once such a help in achieving economic security, is today a hindrance. Until this fact is recognized and the situation re-examined and reinterpreted, the Dakotas will not get very far in the white man's economic world.

Let me show you some of the ways it interferes. Here is a Dakota rancher. He is doing amazingly well. He has choice cattle. He ships them and gets good prices. His white neighbors regard him as their peer. They respect him because he is making money—their criterion of worth. They defer to him, ask his advice, do things cooperatively with him. And everything goes well.

Just when he has some fine sleek steers ready for market, his mother-in-law dies. What does he do? He neglects his shipping program to attend to her funeral. He kills a beef and gives a big feast. The white neighbors are amazed. "Why, the man has gone crazy, stark crazy," they say. "What's the matter with him anyway? See? That's the way of the Indian. He can't stand up long."

They cannot possibly know that Dakota kinship requires the utmost in mutual courtesy between a man and his mother-in-law. His mother-in-law had always treated him as well as he had her. This that he was doing was an indispensable part of the pattern of mutual respect. This has been always so, between son-in-law and mother-in-law. The white man, with his rude and sometimes cruel mother-in-law jokes, cannot understand that.

But the Dakota never explains. What's the use? His neighbors won't understand. He knows what they think of him now; so he avoids them. Perhaps the old camaraderie with them is gone forever. He is left on the outside of business. He never again regains his standing. "All right, I am a Dakota. So what? I have to act as a relative, and it's none of their business."

Here is a man, a Hampton graduate. He comes home with some advanced ideas. He has had a simple course in business. He decides to try his wings. He buys out the local trader and starts in. He would do all right, perhaps, if he were in another community. But now his uncle comes, asking for credit. "Of course." And he even adds, remembering his uncle's great regard for his mother who is now dead, "But, Uncle, you need never pay."

Other relatives come to visit, and his wife takes out food from the shelves to feed them. The account gets mixed up, since she has had no training in such things. Again, one day he invites his cousin and his cousin's family and they quite naturally bring their little ones. He is touched by the presence of his dear cousin who in his youth did many fine things for him. So he says to the wife, "*Hanka* [wife of a brother or cousin], let the children pick out as many candies and cookies as they want." But, being more progressive than most of the women, she appreciates that he is trying to make money. "No, *sic'e*, I can't do that. It is not right to take your stock." But he is all the more stirred by sentiment. "What is all this stock to me," he replies, "if I must deprive my cousin's children of a little pleasure?" And, with a largess that would make a white grocer gulp, he dishes out great fistfuls of sweets for the delighted children.

By and by he realizes that his store is failing, that there are too many leaks in it; so he decides to give up storekeeping and live like the rest. He knows exactly why he has failed. But he does not want to think about it. It is all right in any case. His relatives come first always, he says to himself. He derives a certain satisfaction in not betraying the way of his people.

I knew a very thoughtful, observant, full-blood boy. He was a lovely boy, with considerable character for one so young. He came from a superior Dakota family, headed by a wise grandfather. He was impressed by the success of their Norwegian neighbors, whose ways he watched. They came there with nothing, pushing a cart. They holed into the hillside until they could build a log house. In a few short years they had stock— chickens, geese, ducks, pigs, cows. They made cheese, and the man fished and peddled the cheese and fish in the community. His boys went barefoot, working like men. "They work and keep at it," he thought. "That's why they have things."

He went to the nearest town and watched small business men—bootblacks, harness-makers, tailors— and saw that while they made little they made it daily and lived on less than they made. By and by they would be able to get into something better.

"I can work that hard, too. The celebrations and the other events that boys enjoy don't attract me. I will have a business."

He got his "Sioux benefit" and spent it all on a course in auto mechanics, for that was his bent. He was sometimes homesick in the distant city where he trained, but he did not go home till he finished. Then he set up a little shop back of his home. People brought work to him, though some came without any money to pay for the work. But he was related to them all. He would not dream of saying, "Show me first your money," but went ahead and did their work. Some paid; others, who were obviously too poor, he told not to bother. This was what a Dakota relative should do.

In time he had to close. He was coming down with T.B. anyway. Frustrated, he lay in patient silence and eventually died. He was only one of many Dakotas with longings and ambition who could not earn a living in the white man's way *in a Dakota community.* Those who came to see him wept at his decline. They did not realize what was killing him. It is impossible for the majority to look at their own ways objectively, or for a few to change a deeply embedded and ancient practice, even if they see and would.

Here's another angle to this problem. In olden times people used to travel cross-country to other camp-circles, knowing they had relatives everywhere. It was like going home. Those relatives would see that they didn't starve, for courtesy-food was easily given when everybody could go out and hunt and bring in meat. But things are changed now. People have to work hard by the day for money with which to take care of their own families. Many Dakotas realize this, and so, in order not to inconvenience their friends, they stay home until they can go prepared to meet all their expenses. Nevertheless, there are those yet who haven't thought this through and who still go about, as of old, depending on their relatives. When they went by team, they were always sure to get home somehow. But now (except as prevented by the wartime restrictions on gasoline) they nearly all go by car, and often find themselves unable to buy gas for the return trip or to meet emergencies incidental to car travel. Of course their hosts never let them down in such cases. They provide the return expenses if they can; sometimes they borrow money to do so. Or, if the visitors must stay on awhile, they are welcome, whatever the drain on the family budget. The fact is they are very welcome anyway, for the people love to see their friends at all events. Just the same, the host is bound to suffer. He may speak to others of the demands upon him, not in reproach of his guests for a lack of consideration for him, but rather in reproach of himself that he cannot do all he would like. He blames only himself for inadequacy. "If these had been the days when I was better fixed!" he sighs.

Nowadays this sort of thing often works unequally, for such a host may never visit those guests to enjoy their hospitality. If he did, doubtless they would want to do as much for him and more—they just don't get the chance. I am blaming no one here but only pointing up the difficulties in these times of meeting kinship obligations in the old grand manner.

Today, especially with the boys in the war, loyalty to the demands of kinship is sometimes abused. At celebrations, for instance, some wily singers will without warning break into a stirring old song lauding a famous hero long dead. But instead of the legendary hero's name, they substitute names of the soldier-sons of some of the spectators, hoping to touch them and embarrass them into making gifts in their honor even though they cannot afford them. Many are thus affected, even some who in saner hours disapprove of continuing the ancient practice in these times and who later wish their emotions had not got the best of their better judgment. It is an unfair advantage, in any case, since constant reciprocal giving is no longer possible. Those who thus play on parental emotion are making a good thing for their own benefit out of a once legitimate practice, knowing well enough that they will never have to repay in kind. Unfortunately, such abuses are thus sometimes willfully planned by the unscrupulous in these days of cultural disintegration. Many of the people do not approve these practices. This is especially true of mature and progressive Christians. They see them as a devastating thing.

Yet, on the other hand, a magazine article about Indians in the war, written by the Secretary of the Interior, says:

The religious observances which take place when an Indian boy or girl enters the armed forces give an insight into the philosophical attitude which the Indians bear toward the war. Among the Navajo it is a "sing," among the Dakotas it is a

"give-away." . . . A recent "give-away" took place on the
Port Peck reservation in Montana when Helen Warrior, a
full-blood Sioux and a junior at Montana State College, left
to join the WAC.

That is a most confusing statement. In the first
place, a "give-away" was not a religious practice but
a social custom, and it does not square with conditions
today. Carried to its logical conclusion, it means that
the people may to their advantage continue as of old
to divest themselves of what they own. And today that
simply is not possible. How can such a practice be
condoned at the same time that the government is
spending many thousands of American dollars in helping the Indians achieve economic security? I declare,
I don't get it!

There is still another situation, one in which white
and Dakota ideas about economics are likely to clash—
the transaction of business between the two groups.
Neither understands the other's premise, with the result that all too often the white man gets nearly all and
the Dakota is left "holding the bag." This incident re-
flects the problem better than any exposition of it I
could give.

From our mission a Dakota girl went to work for a
doctor, a friend of her people. She was unaccustomed
to urban life but was ambitious to learn. The doctor
and his wife helped her in every way, and she was doing
all right until the following happened.

"I bought a dress," she told me, "but it did not suit
me, so Mrs. M. advised me to return it. But the owner

of the ready-to-wear shop refused to give me back my money, though I couldn't use the dress and didn't want it. I couldn't understand such an attitude; so I just laid the dress on the counter and walked out without a word."

That man knew where she lived, yet he made no further effort to settle the matter fairly. He kept the dress because she made no fuss. By not making a fuss, she was challenging him to do the right thing. Doubtless he sold the dress again and made a double profit; and doubtless he shrugged a shoulder, thinking, "If she wants to be a sucker, can I help it?"

The Dakota people cannot comprehend such tactics; they are outside their code. Innate courtesy comes first. They would rather lose double any day than profit double at another's expense. Somewhere between the two positions they have to work out an adjustment. How to make it without losing something very fine is the real problem here.

Here is another instance, on a larger scale. In the government magazine *Indians at Work* it was reported that when an army officer asked the Navajos in Arizona for a bombing range, they gave it outright without argument. "If our country needs it, of course . . ." And when the representative of the Indian Office, as their protector, tried to get a good bargain for them, they still did not think primarily of that. Whatever the army thought was right, they said, was right with them.

Now those were Navajos; but they might just as

well have been Dakotas. This forces me to anticipate what I wanted to say later—that the Indian character, point of view, and set of values are pretty much the same, regardless of tribal and language differences. How did they all get that way? I have tried to show how, with reference to the Dakotas. Did it interest you? Maybe a study of the others will be just as interesting, if not more so. By whatever the respective disciplines, the Indians have developed on this continent an ethos that is well-nigh universal, that makes them one in general character, though there are tribal variations.

Now let me cite a similar case among the Dakotas. According to the *Messenger*, a weekly newspaper of Martin, South Dakota, it seems that Dakotas of the Pine Ridge reservation have also turned over a vast territory, just as gladly. They have even removed their homes to give room for a bombing range there and have asked nothing. Will they be paid what the land is worth to the army? Or will they be forgotten again when the war is over? For, therein, too, lies a wide difference between the Dakota way—the Indian way, I may now reasonably say—and the white man's way. Moral obligations, kinship obligations, human courtesy, and self-respect are what motivate good deeds among Indians.

Those Dakotas assume without question that surely so great and honorable a personage as Uncle Sam will do his part—and in a handsome measure, entirely worthy of himself. It would be unthinkable to seem to doubt him, for this, too, was inherent in the old idea: if someone makes me glad with a gift, I am mindful not only of the gift but also of the spirit that prompted him; I am honored by his regard toward me; he gives freely without any provisos to safeguard himself, and thereby he offers me a chance to "play the man," too. My part, therefore, is to make sure my token amply justifies his assumption about me.

But the way of the white men is different—a fact that Indians still have to realize and use when dealing with them. It must be on a strict business basis. It calls for a prior commitment safe from loopholes and for a signature on the dotted line. "If you will do this for me, I will do that for you"; or better yet, "If I do this much for you, how much will you do for me?"

The two ways are at such variance! How will those bombing ranges be recompensed, I am interested to know. Graciously, honorably, and amply? Or will they be ignored and their present indispensable worth played down when they are no longer needed? Time will tell.

To summarize this brief account of what took place in the reservation period: the Dakota people started out with promise in adjusting themselves to a totally different way of life. They were adaptable and realistic in making material changes. Whenever it seemed expedient, they substituted the new for the old without undue sentiment. Their casual shift from travois to wagon and from wagon to motorcar was only one example. It will be just as casual from motorcar to airplane. Just wait and see! Flying has long since lost its novelty for a people whose sons are even now soaring like eagles over every country and ocean of the world.

We saw how and why they were able to make an easy transition when they accepted the new religion, and how they ran into their first real trouble when they went to school. The homeward pull of kinship and filial obligations was what distracted the young Dakotas from their studies, sometimes to their lasting harm. However, this difficulty was destined to disappear gradually as each succeeding generation understood better, from its own school experience, the necessity of uninterrupted education for their children. It was not till they tried to do business that they were hopelessly blocked by the obligatory duties and kinship interdependence of the past that still persisted, hidden but strong.

Yet even that difficulty might have been solved. Of course the people could hardly have been expected to free themselves of their own accord from what was once so fundamental to their corporate life. But, if the missionaries and government officials had studied the problem with the chiefs and leaders, together they might have been able to reinterpret the ideal and revamp the customs in a workable form acceptable to the people. The approach might have been something like this:

"In the past we Dakotas honored each other, principally by expecting help from each other and taking pride in the confidence implicit in that expectation. We did not fail each other. It worked well because we were all in position to act in the same way. Nowadays conditions are different. No longer can we all meet these demands equally. But we may still go on honoring each other in a new way. Still confident of each other's loyalty, we can honor each other by taking pride in helping ourselves, thereby sparing each other undue hardship for our sakes. So shall we still be good relatives."

If the spreading of this idea had been made a universal concern and if their strong leaders—chiefs, chiefs' sons, and native missionaries—had been commissioned to lead their people with sympathy into the new way, the problem could have been solved, I believe. Many Dakota thinkers saw what the trouble was, but they could not start a campaign against it without seeming to deny their own obligations and to be disloyal to the way of their fathers. They needed official sanction, appointment, and moral support, and they did not have it. With certain Dakota leaders calling the signals, they could hardly have missed. A native leadership, unweakened as yet, had it been given free rein— and I do mean free—could have done this and many other great things.

I can almost hear some of those earnest leaders, wonderfully persuasive speakers, stirring their people:

"Come now, our dear relatives, clearly we are up against it. But, as in the past, there is always a way out when our people act together. This that our friends have advised is for our good—but only if we all do it. *Hu-ka-hé!*"

That word *Hu-ka-hé!* was a powerful and compelling cry, unheard, alas, through these many years of hampered initiative. Warriors and other groups used to shout it in unison as a signal to action. It is something like "Let's go, gang!" but much more forceful, implying corporate action by a group bound mystically together to act for the common good; to win; to meet whatever comes, militantly. It is a word aflame with such challenge as no old-time Dakota could resist.

Another major reason for slow progress was that the people were never made to understand in precise terms just *why* they must prepare themselves, and *how;* and *when* they must complete that preparation, and exactly *what* would happen if they failed. Instead, life became a treadmill leading nowhere. That's enough to kill a people's spirit. "They are apathetic," critics say. It's a wonder they are alive to be apathetic. What was the use of learning in school? Where were they going anyway? When would they arrive? If nobody knew the answers, if things were to go on endlessly in the same old way, then why hurry? And in the main, that's how their first fine enthusiasm died, and lethargy set in.

They should have been told over and over and over: "On such and such a date you have to assume your places as American citizens. You can't live like this forever. But, unless you prepare, you will have a bad time of it when that day comes. So, *if you love your children,* get ready, and get them ready, now!"

That last would have been the Achilles heel: they do love their children. If they had really understood what it was all about, I do not think they would have been so detached and listless, content to sit on the shore, idly watching all recent comers to this country launch into the stream of American life and sail gaily past them. As Americans in a unique sense, they too should be right in there!

Many of their troubles might be attributed to such things as lack of education in the value of money and the care of it. The subject remained remote and unrealistic, presupposing a paternalistic government that would handle their money forever, as if they were congenitally incompetent. Until recently the value and use of land was also ignored. For many years the people were under pressure by white buyers to dispose of their land, and they used the money freely, not realizing that it was capital to be invested rather than income to be expended. In this respect they did as any people do who have not had proper training. They have been called improvident when really they were simply inexperienced in a radically different way of life. The majority are still inexperienced. Proper and sufficient education for the American life of today is what our people badly need. It is long overdue. Meantime poverty is all too general, and landlessness is still a haunting fact, in spite of all that the Indian Office is trying to do toward meeting the problem. The results are improper housing, unhealthful conditions, and all the attendant evils that spring up among any people living in such surroundings.

A further word about the religious picture today. We have seen that Christianity took hold quickly among the Dakotas. With phenomenal strides the work advanced and in a short while there were little chapels all over the reservations. But I should not be strictly honest to leave that rosy picture, as though all had been finished. Much work lies ahead. Those dramatic conversions in the early days, those adult baptisms, and those throngs of earnest candidates for confirmation, crowding around the improvised chancel rail—all that was indeed inspiring, comparable to apostolic times.

And yet those were only beginnings. Christianity is a growth; and in a land where numerous difficulties abound to militate against it, to retard or thwart it, its nurture should be watchful and unremitting. Indeed, once planted, it should be helped to expand ever more, to take deeper roots and to put forth more vigorous branches. The call for strong church work in the Indian country increases. The Dakotas and indeed all Indians need the churches, now as never before. May we never forget that.

Part IV

The Present Crisis

14: INDIAN LIFE IN WARTIME

IN SPITE OF LAUDABLE EFFORTS PUT FORTH TO HELP the Indians along and rehabilitate them, only a small minority have been reached so far. There are countless families in the remote pockets of reservations still in great poverty. Anyone who drives through their country can see it. The clergy who minister to their spiritual wants see it constantly. Visitors, students of sociology, evaluators and surveyors of the reservation situation come away depressed by the shabbiness and drabness of existence surrounding many families and the general apathy and passivity that pervade the whole picture.

I do not minimize, by failing to dwell on it, all that our churches and our government have done in offering higher education for the young people. Many of them have made a success that is outstanding and are now out working and receiving incomes commensurate with those earned by young people of other races for similar work. But I am talking only of the reservation—of the homes from which these individuals have gone forth and of the state of mind and the outward appearance of the majority of their people. Life on the reservation has always been seemingly inactive. The people have rarely had very much, sometimes nothing, and many homes are dismal and the life in them is listless by contrast with the homes of the white settlers. It is no wonder that these homes have provoked harsh comments from superficial observers. "Look at their homes! Those people certainly have no initiative," critics said of them, and stopped there, not curious enough to find out *why*. "They are beggars," some said with more harshness than judgment. "They wait only on the government and accept charity without shame."

But they were wrong who said that. To the older people, especially, it was not charity. Don't you see, it was part of that same old ideal of interdependence expressed in giving. It was right that Uncle Sam should help the Indians. They were poor, made poor through circumstances they could not control. It was Uncle Sam's duty to show himself a man in that way. They could not return the compliment now, maybe never. But if ever a time came when they could, they would not be found wanting. Nor were they, for a time *did* come.

As soon as our country became involved in war, the Indians of all tribes got into action. They did it in 1917 and they did it again and in fuller measure in

1941 and the years following. Who can say they are
apathetic and listless now? They have something to
bestir themselves about at last—what a pity it had to
be a war! And it has called forth all those dormant
qualities that had been thought killed long ago—initiative, industry, alertness. And they had generally retained their infinite patience, sympathy, gentleness,
religious devotion, tolerance, showing an amazing lack
of bitterness—amazing, because they have had plenty
to be bitter about. They are not bitter, not because
they are childish and don't know enough to be, but
because they are wise. They know that bitterness en-
dangers dignity—another inalienable trait—and solves
nothing. A number of Indian men were listening to an
impassioned broadcast calling Hitler and Tojo all sorts
of ugly names. Presently one of them shook his head.
"They shouldn't say that!" was the only comment he
made, but nothing more was needed to show his feelings.

All the Indians today may be thought of as divided
into the same three groupings found among any other
class of citizens—those who are left at home, the men
and women in the services, and the workers in war industries. Let me tell you about them.

First, some glimpses of the people at home, who
carry on there, praying, working, and comforting one
another as they meet the inevitable hardships and sor-
rows that come to all in war. I receive many letters
from my Dakota kith and kin telling me what goes on
among that particular tribe. One says quite naturally,

in speaking of a recent drive from Rosebud to Rapid
City, "Of course it was a long slow ride in the cold, at
thirty-five miles an hour, but we made it all right." I
know that road. It is long, monotonous, and deserted.
Nobody on earth would ever know if they speeded
along, as usual, at fifty miles an hour. But they had
been asked not to do so in order to conserve gas and
tires for the sake of the boys; so they obeyed. It was
not smart to cheat.

Then I have the story of a woman whose only son
was the first from that reservation to be killed in action. In her intense grief, she reverted to ancient custom, so long given up, and demeaned herself by cutting
off her hair, wearing her oldest clothes, and wandering
over the hills, wailing incessantly. Nor would she be
comforted. Did the people do anything? Certainly. In
the old-time manner, which they now carry over into
their church, they made a feast and invited the be-
reaved mother. After a memorial service in the church
they went down to the guild hall. There the elder men
and women, strong in their faith and given to such
exhortation, made speeches addressed to her, as is the
traditional manner of condoling with those who mourn.
"I do not presume to make light of your great sorrow,
my relative," said one earnest Christian woman, "but
to remind you of God's love." And so the woman's
silent weeping subsided. They washed her tear-stained
face and partook of food with her, all in decent quiet,
for this was a ceremony. "Then they all collected gifts
for her, mostly food," the letter ends, "and she told

them she felt lots stronger now because they had talked to her and comforted her."

Another letter tells what happened after a four-engined bomber burst into flames high over a little Dakota chapel and fell blazing and crashing to the ground not far off. Everyone in it was lost. The Dakota catechist immediately rang the bell and the people came running. When he saw that all hope of rescue was gone he said to them, "My relatives, let us go into the church." They took their places, some weeping softly for the nameless victims. Then he read prayers from the burial office in the native tongue amid a stillness that was absolute but for the fire still crackling outside. The families of the boys in that plane might like to know that prayers were offered for them first by Christian Dakotas.

In no line of any letter is there the least sign of discouragement or despondency over their hardships. The people see singly: "There's a job to be done. So let's get at it. Never mind about *us* now."

Next, the second group: the young men and women in the services. The reports come thick and fast about them and their record shows that they are more than doing their best. They are constantly being cited for heroism and given the various army and navy decorations. The Secretary of the Interior, Harold L. Ickes, writes of them:

The inherited talents of the Indian make him uniquely valuable. He has endurance, rhythm, a feeling for timing, coordination, sense perception, an uncanny ability for getting over any kind of terrain at night, and, better than all else, an enthusiasm for fighting. He takes a rough job and makes a game of it. Rigors of combat hold no terrors for him; severe discipline and hard duties do not deter him.

That is a generous and, I believe, fair appraisal, but for one word that may strike a false note, "an enthusiasm for fighting." For me that flavors too much of the old notion of savage bloodthirstiness, consciously or unconsciously imputed indiscriminately to all Indians. It does not seem a fair way to represent modern Indian boys who had known only peace. "An enthusiasm for action when the aim is plain" would be truer.

I see a little paper each month, *Victory News*, edited by a talented Dakota girl, an A.B. from Carleton College. Her staff are all Dakotas. It is mimeographed by them on the reservation and is the organ of the Victory Club of Rosebud, through which the people work together to send cheer and home news to the boys all over the world. Think of it, a little Indian paper with a mailing list that covers the globe! There are similar papers at other places. These clubs prepare army kits and write personal letters to the boys without parents and to those whose parents cannot write.

Here are a few random excerpts from service men's letters, which *Victory News* quotes monthly:

Pfc. Anthony Omaha-Boy is "glad for God's protection." Pfc. Laverne Iron Wing is studying French and Italian between times! Robert Schmidt is a gunner on one of Uncle Sam's flying forts. Sgt. Gilbert

Feather asks "that we all pray God to bring us safely back to the good old U.S.A." Pvt. Albert Bad Hand ends, "I haven't seen my Indian pals since I came over. I am aching to see one so that I can chat with him in Dakota."

The *Martin Messenger Weekly*, of Martin, South Dakota, carried this letter from Paddy Starr, in Hawaii, addressed to his catechist. It shows that the boys feel responsible for their home church: "You may think I have forgotten everything back home. No. I bear every one of you in my heart. I'm enclosing a money order for $15.00, of which $5.00 is for the Men's Society, $5.00 for the Women's Auxiliary, and $5.00 for the Young People's Fellowship. I'm doing my part over here. In prayers I want every one of you to do your part."

Indian boys are in every branch of service. From General Tinker, who lost his life at the very start of the war, down to the last private, they qualify for any post and are serving everywhere, courageously.

Indian girls are Red Cross nurses, WACS, and WAVES. They, too, are everywhere. When a missionary's wife asked where his sister was now, a little full-blood boy answered quite casually, "In Iceland." Iceland was now part of his world.

These new experiences of Indian youth raise some vital questions about their training, and this may be a good place to stop and consider them.

Before the war some of the educational planning was directed to a very special kind of life. It was predicated on the common statement, "Ninety per cent of the Indians return to the reservation anyway," the assumption always being that there is little need of training them for the outside world since they will not be in it. The course of study and training was thus devised for the limited, expectable needs of reservation life. And now, see where the young people are! How well prepared were they for the world at large? It seemed a good idea at the time, no doubt. But in future a course of study that corresponds in all essentials to the requirements of the various state boards of education might be safer—and fairer to the Indians in the long run.

We might well ask ourselves, "Why do they return to the reservation, anyway?" Well, partly it is that pull toward home and family, a universal human need but peculiarly accentuated in the Indian nature from centuries of close family and clan and *tiyośpaye* life. But that is not all. It is also because Indian young people had not been prepared to get into American general society and feel at home in it. If they had known the ordinary, commonplace things that other American youth take for granted, they would not have felt ill at ease and lonely there. If one is not familiar with the allusions and casual references that pepper the conversation of a particular group, one is bound to feel left out. Indian people are by nature reticent and retiring; when they feel a lack of social ease and self-confidence, they want to run away from the crowd, knowing they are ill-prepared to hold their own. It is

not enough to be a good mechanic or a well trained
stenographer at such times.

I sometimes listen to quiz programs on the radio to
see if I can answer the questions. It challenges me to
find out the things I miss. I don't like *not* to know the
answers. Some Americans know them; why not I? That
is the way I think other Indians feel. That is how some
parents have been feeling of late. They have been saying they want their children to learn what the other
children in their state are required to learn. They can
teach them all the Indian lore and language they themselves choose, they say, and do a better job of it. They
want the schools to concentrate on things the children
cannot learn at home. I think they have something
there.

The war has indeed wrought an overnight change in
the outlook, horizon, and even the habits of the Indian
people—a change that might not have come about for
many years yet. For weal or woe, the former reservation life has been altered radically. As it looks now,
that idea of a special course of study set up for Indians
alone shows up a bit negatively as a kind of race dis-
crimination. What is right and necessary for the majority of American school children and is made available to them ought not to be denied to other American
children. It is a challenge, moreover, to be expected to
measure up, the same as anyone else, rather than to
have allowances continually made on the basis of race.

The third group we are considering here, the workers in industry, are numerous and important. Whole

families have moved into the cities and are meeting problems they have never faced before. As workers they are valuable. Skillful with their hands at tasks requiring meticulous care, they are extremely accurate, patient, dependable. If they are a split second more deliberate than some others, they make correspondingly fewer mistakes that might prove fatal. They will not stop to bargain for themselves; it is not in their tradition to think of self first; and they will not grumble. They will never do anything to hinder the war effort. They are too peculiarly American for that.

One of their problems is that of paying rent. They find it an irksome concomitant to living away from their own homes. They have never paid rent before. Naturally they try to find the least expensive places— with the result that they sometimes find themselves among undesirable neighbors. And of course there are numerous other problems. What to do with their children and adolescent girls in these surroundings is one of the hardest problems. How to get wholesome entertainment is another, and where to go to church, a third.

These Indians are earning "big money" now, and for many of them it is their first experience. They like it and will want to keep on earning and being able to buy, out of their own efforts entirely, what they desire, instead of waiting endlessly for their money from leases handled by the agency.

But do they all know how to take care of their money? What knowledge have they of practical business? Can they budget wisely? Many of them have till now had little chance to handle money, since the agency office has always managed even personal accounts for the majority of them.

And then what of the great problem they share with peoples on every continent—the new ordering of their life when their sons and daughters return from the armed services and the war industries are closed?

What will the workers in war plants do then? Many will doubtless want to stay in the cities, having become urbanized and liking it. Some will doubtless get on there; but others may quite possibly be forced out of work. Reticent and uncompetitive, as some of their tribal societies have made their people, perhaps they will have their jobs snatched by the aggressive and blatant type of workers who are used to competition.

The vast majority will probably want to go home. It is natural to want to be near one's own people. Many Indians cannot yet feel complete with just their little family, their spouse and children. They have been used to thinking in terms of the larger family groups for many generations. Even while they work their hearts turn homeward. "This is transitory," they think. "We will soon be home again." For many, that means the reservation, and it seems very good to them, however drab and bare it may look to outsiders. It will be good to get into their own homes, be they ever so humble. At least they won't have to feel beholden to landlords and will be able once again to reckon without rent. Owning one's own home will take on a new meaning.

The boys and girls in distant lands must be thinking

of home, too. Perhaps for the first time they really appreciate having lands and houses. Their own sojourn in areas of great destruction where they see throngs of pitiful refugees will make them extra thankful for America and for their reservation homes.

Numbers of these young people will want to get back and do something about the life in their old communities. For now they have seen things, not only pitiful but also thought-provoking things: how people get along; how they work without letup to improve their places; how they manage to own some livestock and take good care of it; and how they grow things on every spare inch of ground and garner every berry and grain, loath to lose even one. Wonderful object lessons! Those who have been away will want to copy them when they come home.

Being with other people is indeed an eye opener to many things. The boys and girls have had a chance to see how they measure up in the life of average American communities, and they have begun to realize what their churches and schools have done for them. They went to school in the past because it seemed they must, and they occupied themselves with whatever was taught them. They had no choice about it; but then they had no basis for making a choice anyway. Some of it has certainly stood them in good stead, but other parts of it looks now like so much waste. They might have learned certain other things, instead, for which they now feel a definite lack. They know now, too, that they never went far enough in any one thing, nor deep enough into fundamentals. That was why they disqualified for this or that type of specialized training, even though they knew they could do it because they had a natural feel for it.

They will come back with perspective. They will see their churches and their schools in a new light. They will appreciate what those agencies have tried to do for them. Now they will be able to say just what they require of them. There will be a new call to government to help them with their land and economic problems, since they will be ready and eager for help. There will be a new call for the schools, for now they know what they need, what they missed in the past, and what their children must not miss in the future. They have fought and suffered for their country. They are Americans, and they will want to be treated as such. They will want to be able to talk the common language of America, and I don't mean just literally, but figuratively as well. That is to say, they will want to participate in the larger thought and life of the land and not be given special work scaled down to their abilities, as if those abilities were static, or to their needs, as if those needs must always be limited to tribal life. Tribal life is only a phase in human development anyway. The next step, for every people, is national life. Usually that is a slow process; but in the case of the Indians it needn't be, since national life pervades the very atmosphere they breathe. The schools must help them adjust to it.

But that's not all. Far and above all that government can do and that the school can do lies the peculiar contribution of the church. If the Indians need the government to help them materially and the schools to help them mentally, they need the church, even more, to help them spiritually. As interdependent as these three agencies are and as essential as they all are, the church's part is the *sine qua non* of them all. For it is to the church they must look for strength to withstand temptation, wisdom to make right choices, steadfastness to see things through, and hope and faith in the eventual victory of right. Without the church and her nurturing, the Indian people will not be able to get the most and the best out of all the fine things that may be offered by government and by education in the years ahead. This I believe unqualifiedly.

Nobody knows and appreciates the fact any more than Indians themselves that there were splendid disciplines in the old culture to sustain and strengthen its people. But we have to be realistic enough to admit that, in an alien setting, and increasingly as time goes on, those disciplines lose their force. This is true particularly with the younger Indians when they venture out beyond their reservation boundaries. It is not bulwark enough then that they know their skill and trade so well that they can get along economically, for they still have needs that the best money-making knowledge cannot supply. Because they are few and scattered, they can be terribly lonely in their new environment, without friends to help them to find their way around and to fit into their community's life.

We know how impossible it is for a white man to crash a lodge or club of even his own kind of people, speaking his language and thinking as he thinks. He must have friends already inside to introduce him and give him moral support. Then how much more do people of an alien background, tongue, and thought-patterns need a friend! That friend is logically the church. No other institution is so well equipped to offer friendship, sympathy, wise counsel, and unselfish assistance to all who need it. Also it is the one single institution that is already familiar to young Indians venturing out. In times of stress back home they turned to their missionaries; what is more natural than for them to look to the church when they are in new and strange places?

Loyalty and trust, yes, and love cannot be bought or coerced; they have to be won. And, as far as I can see, it has always been the church more than any secular agency that has won these from the Indians, through continuous unselfish and personal service. It is their friend. No wonder they look to it wherever they find it, expecting it still to be their friend.

15: TOWARD THE NEW COMMUNITY

I HAVE BEEN TALKING ON ABOUT INDIANS THROUGH many pages, and some of the things I have said will doubtless be forgotten. If they are, it will be because they have not been put vividly enough to be retained; therefore they deserve to be forgotten. But this much that I say in closing I wish might stick.

The Indians' progress has been slow and discouraging at times; but *there are reasons why.* I never hear a speaker who tells about the depressing aspects of the problem in detail and then stops there, but that I want to ask, "Why?" For the American people need to understand *why,* so that they will not blame the people unduly, as if there were something congenitally wrong with them, but will understand the causes. I have tried to indicate what they are, for one tribe, and how they might be removed so that the people can go ahead unhindered. I have suggested that other tribes who have elements in their tradition that impede their progress might be helped to discover what they are and how to deal with them intelligently and constructively.

Part of the apathy and hopelessness apparent among Indians may sometimes be due to the absence of a clear plan. Without being really impressed with the urgency of their achieving full readiness to participate in American life, they have been carried along throughout the many decades of their history. They have never been aroused and deeply stirred to get ready by any special time, for any special thing, in any special way. Their life has been separated by a wide gulf from that of all other Americans.

To quote John Stuart Mill, "a state which dwarfs its men in order that they may be more docile instruments in its hands *even for beneficial purposes* will find that with small men no great thing can really be accomplished." (The italics are mine.) In a way, I believe that this is what has happened to the Indian people. They have always been so supervised and so taken care of that it has been hard to "try their wings" without self-consciousness. And they have been so remote from general American life that they don't always know what to try.

"Very well," you say, "if that's all, it can be taken care of." But not so fast. That isn't all. Unfortunately these many decades of paternalism and protection and gratuity have left their mark. That is not so strange, nor is such a result peculiar to Indians. Have we not in our own time seen how spoiled and weakened people may become with a little of that sort of thing? So, along with all the other problems is that of re-education, this time for eventual qualification for full citizenship with all its duties and responsibilities as well as all its privileges.

It will take time, but with a definite end in plain view and with consistent hammering at the job of getting ready, tribe by tribe, I believe it can be accomplished. In the old days the Indians had dignity and pride. They still do. An appeal to their pride, their manhood, their tribehood, would bring a response. But they must be approached with dignity and sincerity, and told earnestly by their friends that here is a profoundly critical, essential task for them all to unite on *for the good of their children.* I am optimistic enough to think they would respond, especially if they are told to go ahead *in their own way*—that too is important—

and if a chance is given them to do this without a kind
of stifling oversight.

Of course they will need a lot of help: from the government, which has really done a great deal for them—
I am mindful of that, especially in saving their lands
and improving their health through hospitals and pre-
ventive measures; and continued help also from the
churches, which have stood by them from the first.
May I suggest a few ways in which this help can be
administered?

Here, for instance, is one matter of great importance
to the Indians in making contacts with the outside
world, something which might easily have been attended to long ago. Persons with very involved descrip-
tive names might have been helped to simplify them.
"Runs-Close-to-the-Village," "Comes-Home-Alive,"
"Walks-under-the-Ground," and scores of others—
what kind of names are those for modern boys and girls
to bear in general society? Such students cannot stand
up to recite in public schools and colleges without the
class snickering impolitely. What do you think the
effect of that is on them, even if they know all the
answers?

If friends of the Indian people had investigated and
understood these "names," it would have been found
that they are not "names" at all as we know them. They
are oral records, invented by people who did not write,
for the purpose of keeping fresh in the tribal memory
great deeds and striking experiences out of their history. They do not refer to persons bearing these names

today. In Dakota, you do not say, if you are idiomatically correct, "What is your name?" but, "In what manner do they say of you?" That means, "According to what deed are you known?" The deed of an ancestor was memorialized in a phrase applied to a descendant of his. Such a one was really an engraved memorial tablet walking around! This deed was suggested in a few words, and your imagination filled in the story, or you could always ask what the exact reference was. Someone is known as "Runs-Close-to-the-Village." This might simply epitomize the following: A warrior once in broad daylight dared to run along a row of enemy tipis, so defiantly close that anyone might have shot him, yet his foes were too stunned by his rare courage to do so. By the incredibility of his nerve he came through alive. So his great-nephew bears his record, "Runs-Close-to-the-Village." Names were provocative of gifts, and closely allied to the "give-away" custom. Whenever such a name was called aloud it stirred up fresh glory in a past deed and the relatives gave away gifts. One must not speak them casually without giving a gift. Kinship terms were used instead.

But in the period when the government was assuming the direction of Indian affairs, the interpreters, having no knowledge of all this background for Indian names, made inadequate and clumsy translations of the terms. Some were not even accurate. And they are not surnames; they are references borne individually. Why must boys and girls have to bear them forever as family names?

Consider the case of "One-Skunk," for instance. He volunteered for the first commando raid on France. Yet the publicity he received was not primarily because he was a brave American but because his Indian name was humorous, not to say ludicrous. Radio commentators had a field day over it. Why was he called that? I do not know, but anyone versed in the ethnology of such matters can hazard a safe enough guess as to the reference. Quite likely that animal played a part in some religious ancestor's vision experience.

But who in a fast-moving army can stop to learn the reference and allow for it? The titter at daily roll call can well be imagined. A soldier might have the qualities of a MacArthur or an Eisenhower, but could he ever demonstrate them with a name like One-Skunk? Many Indian boys, I am sure, have potentialities for leadership and rank but hold back because people laugh at their names. Some simplification, or even the adoption of the father's Christian name to be carried from now on as the family surname, would help tremendously to give the children dignity. Foreign-born Americans can change their names at the drop of a hat; why can't Indians whose names provoke ridicule be helped to do so?

Our educators, and even our churches, have failed in not sensing the psychological effects of such experiences on the young, and investigating and remedying this simple matter. I have detected the semblance of a smile on even such kindly persons as missionaries when they repeated certain names for city audiences.

At once apologetic and amused they were; but I have never heard of anyone being concerned enough to say, "Here is a real handicap—let's remove it."

And what about religious education? People can understand the human verities on which the churches found their whole ministry—kindness, sincerity, truth, love, reverence, sacrifice. Those are invincible when given glowing expression in life.

But the Indians differ from the average American in that their upbringing, outlook, and habits of thought have been distinctive. Therefore, until an education like that of other people is better acquired by them, the methods used for reaching the white population are not always valid for them. This is so particularly of the adults with limited education or none at all. "It goes in the city churches; it must go here, too," we say. So we sometimes load our people down with scores of leaflets, new schemes, and numerous devices that confuse more than they help. Methods have to be adapted for them still. It is quite possible that, as devices come faster than they can be accepted, and newer schemes follow each other at too rapid a pace, bewilderment may result in a paralysis of action, and mission work may bog down. The making of Christians is not dependent upon clever schemes and the continual revising of texts, although we must all recognize how valuable such work is in achieving the larger ends.

Again, our churches need to conserve their adult man power. What's the use of bringing children in and then neglecting them when they are adults? Too often

I have seen well meaning white workers armed with the "latest" methods so feverishly corralling the children for this or that event at a religious gathering that they do not see the grownups, who could be a downright asset. The grownups, too, have had training in their youth and secretly yearn to exercise it still. Many adults sing very well. Why not an inspiring adult choir with voices strong enough to lead, instead of always some timid, sweet, piping, and ineffective little voices? It sounds dear, but a choir has a job to do. I have worked in pageantry a lot, and I know how adults feel. They are too courteous and self-effacing to push themselves, but they will almost invariably take a part assigned them, and do a grand thing with it. You have to understand them.

Please don't think I decry work with children; I rate it high. But the neglect of adult ability always distresses me. Such slighting of adults adds up to an assumption that Indians can't advance, and that the continuing education will never in time help them to their feet, to go it alone. Instead, we seem to start afresh with each generation, thus offsetting what previous workers have done. I know that children who see their parents also doing things and assuming leadership get a new respect for them, take pride in them, and are inspired to try all the harder themselves.

Here's what I mean, in a single illustration: In 1892, a double-text service-book was made in which for some reason the Psalms were numbered with Roman numbers! But, don't you know, by the time I was able to follow the service, nobody had any trouble turning to them for responsive reading. Out of necessity they had learned to read Roman numerals. Yet not so long ago I attended an old church with a long tradition of churchmanship behind it. The white missionary interrupted himself at each juncture of the service to stop to tell the people where to turn next. They knew all the time—or should have. That church had been holding services for half a century, and if what the people learned from year to year had been pooled and conserved, this couldn't have happened.

All this is perpetual guardianship of a sort, too. It presupposes a static mind on racial lines. Not only is our government guilty of marking time with our Indians; our churches often unconsciously do exactly the same thing. Let's face it, and start correcting it now.

In some places the people sense a tendency to move native leaders to lower posts and to put white men in the most responsible places. When that happens, it is discouraging and disappointing to the people as a whole, who naturally feel it is because of their race. It has an unfortunate effect on their pride and morale, and it lessens their enthusiasm. Years ago, for example, strong native ministers held key positions with marked success. But then gradually white supervision was extended over their fields until now very few such native leaders are to be found. The explanation? "It was all right in the old days, when they were all Indians; now that there are so many whites in the Indian country we have to put in men who can deal with both." That is not valid; that is not the solution. Indians or whites, it ought to make no difference, if only their education is comparable. The solution is not to keep Indian leaders forever in subordinate places, but to educate them further. Many have the ability. It has been demonstrated in certain unmistakable cases. Above all, they have the confidence and understanding of the Indian people, an advantage not to be ignored. And, those who are the right material and have sufficient education can and do gain the confidence of white people in their field as well.

Sixty years ago there were some enthusiastic converts, chiefs and such, who organized a Christian brotherhood. They said, "We will form the nucleus of leadership. We know our people's ways and the methods by which they can best be led into civilization. We are Christians. We will invite any Christian who wants to join us."

It was a noble and promising step and entirely native. The other Protestant churches in the field also had promising leaders. At the outset they were invited and came in. They were all relatives anyway. This was church unity in the rough. They had great times and they did great things. They were the liaison officers for the early churches. There's no telling how they might have served both church and government as well as their people.

No telling—since their potential strength, unfortunately, has never to this day been appraised at its true worth; their power with their own people has never been sufficiently exploited, nor have they been encouraged to extend their influence. Yet they have carried on these fifty years and more by themselves. They have been a silent tower of strength among their people. They could be the dynamo if ever a revival of activity were indicated. The members give to good works—to widows and orphans and others—in the traditional manner. But also they are the very first group that has sensed the serious need for regular public school education for their children and have gone ahead to do something about it.

The brotherhoods, moreover, have been sensitive to the need for religious nurture. They asked whether certain mission schools, closed for lack of funds, might not be opened again, and they pledged money as an earnest of their desires. They themselves, all Indians, men and women, have decided this thing on their own initiative. Notice that this thought did not spring in any haphazard fashion from the minds of individual Indians scattered here and there, but that it came out of an *organization.* As they gathered in its meetings its members were free to talk constructively together about their people's deeper needs.

The Indian people—or any people—are a living plant. They must develop naturally, and, as they do, they drop off the lowest petals that have become dried up and useless and are hanging by a single fiber thread. Only the plant knows when to drop them in its development of ever better and fuller bloom at the top. To insist and make it the laudable thing to keep to Indian customs, even when they are outgrown, or, on the other hand, to want results so fast that the happy use of Indian languages and the vestiges of customs, good or bad, are discouraged, wholesale, is to hurt the Indian plant seriously.

The care of one plant is a glorious work, and there is satisfaction in helping it to fruition. The nurture of a whole race to its fulfillment should be worth the very best efforts of all concerned. For real nurture, each distinct group has to be checked for those elements surviving from the past that hinder its growth. I have always believed that general, over-all methods were not the best way, that the life of each tribe needed to be studied for its peculiar characteristics and for those circumstances that seem to be obstacles in its path of development. And now I know that is so.

The church gets close to the people. It can sit down with them in a way that government cannot. In the interest of a whole race, it would be well if church and government could sit down together in their common concern for the Indian people. Together, in understanding openly achieved, they would know better what they were all working for and be able to direct the people to a responsible goal.

I have in mind two pictures. One is of a dying man, the last of the aborigines of America. Frustrated once again, apathetic for keeps this time, he is glad enough to die now because help had not come when his enthusiasm was at one moment re-aroused after long years of dullness—a moment when he was ready for action and needed friends dreadfully and desperately. It is all over now but the final gasp. That would be a fine picture to go into the record of a nation proclaiming the Four Freedoms to the world—for the liberation of all conquered people, except the one it itself had conquered!

The other is a scene borrowed from the Mexican movie, *The Forgotten Village*, by John Steinbeck. The doctors are operating in their weird masks and their white gowns. Up in the balcony sit hundreds of Indian medical students, all in white, with eyes shining and faces alert and eager. Leaning earnestly over the rail, they watch every move. They want to know all about it. They *must* know. They have been told and they accept just what things they must do to save their people. Under compulsion that cannot be resisted, there they are. It is a picture full of promise and hope, of life and growth, of richness and spiritual satisfaction, because it has vision. To put the prophet's negative word in the positive, "Where there is vision, the people live." They are made rich in the things of the spirit, and then, as the logical next step, they are rich in human life.

There is an undeniable choice here. Which picture shall it be? The picture of despair or the picture of hope?

There is no alternative. Now that the people know what they need and want, they are going to be disillusioned, forever this time, if they cannot have it.

Only their friends can help them; and they must. The old Indian fatalism said, "Since it must be so, it is so"; and the result was a passive acceptance, a stoical resignation. But that must go now. From here on, the progression must be rapid: what can be, ought to be; what ought to be, shall be!

And only a people motivated by spiritual power and committed to the teachings of the Master can help bring the right thing to pass.